DEVELOPING, PRINTING & ENLARGING SIMPLIFIED

A MODERN PHOTOGUIDE

DEVELOPING, PRINTING & ENLARGING SIMPLIFIED

by

The Amphoto Editorial Board

AMPHOTO
Garden City, New York 11530

CONTENTS

INTRODUCTION

Darkroom work is one of the most fascinating and creative aspects of photography. Mastering the techniques of processing films and making enlargements lies within the capabilities of even the beginning photographer. Perfecting those techniques to a level of darkroom mastery requires time and patience but the effort is well rewarded. The skilled darkroom worker can truly control the effect and look of his photograph through to the final stages.

This book deals with the fundamentals of darkroom work. It is designed to serve only as an introduction to the subject. However, the effort has been made to include all those basic considerations and skills necessary to set up a working darkroom, develop films, and make successful prints. Sequence and comparison pictures are included to help you better understand the techniques described. Because of the demands of space, color processing has not been included.

Many photographers, having mastered the fundamentals of darkroom work, wish to progress to special printing effects. Again, space has made it impossible to open the Pandora's box of so-called "creative" darkroom work in this volume. However, a special section, "The Creative Darkroom," is included in another Modern Photoguide, *Photographic Tricks.*

This book and certain other titles in the series have been prepared under the supervision of Patricia Maye, Managing Editor of Amphoto. Ms. Maye also designed the book. Amphoto editors, Sheldon Czapnik, Judy Kiviat, and Penny J. Schwartz, cooperated on the text editing and Amphoto Editor-in-Chief John C. Wolf contributed his photographic knowledge and helpful comments.

No matter where you live, you can have your own darkroom. The choice is yours—the bare necessities for developing an occasional roll of film and making contact prints, or an elaborate affair complete with air conditioning and temperature control. The size and extent of your darkroom is both a matter of convenience and personal preference.

The apartment dweller, or other occasional photo finisher, will be satisfied with a simple outfit that can be set up quickly in a small space and then can be disassembled easily. If you do your darkroom work at night, as most people do, you won't even have much trouble making your darkroom dark—a blanket, or other cover, hung over the window is often sufficient.

The usual places for the beginner's photo darkroom are the family kitchen or bathroom, as they provide the running water that is necessary for preparing chemicals and washing films and prints. If the kitchen or bathroom can be completely darkened for handling film, so much the better, but this is not always so easy. Remember, there has to be total darkness for handling film. This means there should be no light leaking through cracks around doors or windows.

It is usually easier for the beginner to start out using one of the "daylight" developing tanks. Some of these can be loaded in ordinary room light; others require total darkness for loading the film into the tank. Many times a closet will do for this job, since it only takes a short time to insert the roll of film into the developing tank. Just make sure there is total darkness in the closet. Use it only at night, with all the room lights turned off and the closet door shut. Another handy method is the changing bag. With one of these, you can load a roll of film into the tank in ordinary room light. After the film is in the tank, the tank is removed from the lighttight bag and the rest of the developing can be done with no fearing of the film being fogged by stray light.

This leaves the biggest problem of darkroom planning—the selection of a space for making prints. Kitchens and bathrooms are the most obvious improvised darkrooms, but almost any space large enough to hold the trays and enlarger will suffice. It is not even necessary to have running water right at the scene of operations. Fixed prints can be stacked temporarily in a tray of water, then carried to the bathtub or sink for washing. Many fine quality prints have been made in an attic, basement, or other converted rooms.

After you have selected the location for your darkroom, sit down and do a little planning to organize for greatest efficiency. Organization, especially in a permanent darkroom, leads to a working pattern which will improve your technique and, in turn, your pictures. Even the simplest darkroom should be planned as to the availability of electrical outlets, handy location of shelf or table space for the enlarger, chemical trays, and darkroom accessories.

Even though your basic equipment may be limited, keep in mind that you may later on develop a greater interest in your hobby. As you become more interested in photography you might want to expand. If provisions for expansion are taken into consideration at the beginning, it will be much easier later on.

If space is available, you might find it easy to partition off a room. The basement is the most likely place to offer space for building a darkroom. Since it will normally be protected from weather, a completely finished wall is not always necessary. Any material can be used if it will make a suitable shield to keep out stray light.

If you are starting from scratch, be sure to place your darkroom near plumbing and electrical outlets to eliminate as much piping and wiring as possible. A linoleum or tile floor covering, especially over a concrete floor, is easy to keep clean and dustless, and is comfortable to stand on during long sessions of developing and printing. If you use Masonite, Formica, or similar smooth, easy-to-clean material for counter tops, water and solution can be quickly wiped off and will not leave damp spots or stains.

Be sure to provide adequate ventilation. Photo chemicals are not generally considered harmful, but if the user works in a stuffy room over open trays of chemicals for long periods of time, it could be dangerous.

In the basement darkroom, you may have a problem that generally is not found anywhere else. That is the problem of too much moisture. This will only be apparent during the summer when the humidity is higher than usual. If you have a large basement with plenty of ventilation, the humidity may not be objectionable; but in a small enclosed room it can be bad enough to ruin some of your equipment and materials. A dehumidifier removes this risk.

When planning your darkroom you should take into consideration the facilities necessary for heating or cooling the room in different seasons. Air conditioners are fine for the summer, but there are other methods of satisfactorily cooling your room. One is to work only at night, when the temperature is usually lower. In the winter, small space heaters can usually provide adequate heat. There are certain types of air conditioners that can be used as coolers in summer and as heat pumps in winter.

Don't overlook the importance of making your darkroom as comfortable as possible to work in. All sinks and work tables should be at a comfortable height. If you are constantly bending over while you are working, you will tire easily and your work won't be enjoyable.

Order in the darkroom is a must for top efficiency. At the very beginning it is best to cultivate the habit of keeping everything in its place. It will be easier than you realize, once you are aware of how you can use all the space available in your darkroom.

First of all, find a space for storing each piece of equipment. If it is always kept in this space, it will be easily found when needed, thus saving time. Your own methods will be dictated by your particular working habits. Take a little time to plan for sensible storage.

Keep your chemicals separated. Chemicals in powdered form should be stored well above and away from areas where water or liquid chemicals are likely to splash into them.

Put each darkroom item in its particular spot, and always return it to this spot. This will help you when you must locate it in the dark. Paper should be handy to the enlarger to prevent needless steps while printing—in a drawer, on a shelf, or special storage box.

Negative filing is important. Ready-made filing envelopes can be bought, as well as filing boxes, although you might have suitable files already on hand in the form of plain envelopes and shoe or cigar boxes.

Various darkroom accessories can be hung around the darkroom using many ordinary items found in the darkroom or around the home. Don't overlook pegboard. The walls of some professional darkrooms are almost completely covered with pegboard, which is used for storing everything from developing reels to dodging implements. One of the most practical places to hang a piece of pegboard is on the darkroom door, which would ordinarily be completely wasted space. Try to hang dodging tools near the enlarger, reels near the sink, and so forth.

Shelf space will be more and more useful as you branch out in your darkroom projects. You don't have to be an expert carpenter to make shelves. Ready-made brackets can be bought for mounting on the wall. Whatever space is available under the enlarger bench or processing table should also be utilized.

The thought of complicated formulas and weights and measures might scare you at first. The truth is that the chemical mixing end of photography has been modernized and is now sometimes simpler than making a cake. All the chemicals needed for turning out finished negatives and prints are available in prepared liquid or powder form; all you have to do is mix them with the right amounts of water. And the number of chemicals you'll need is so small that you'll use very little storage space.

All manufacturers give directions for mixing chemicals on their packages. Always read these instructions carefully, and make sure you understand them. Don't think that one reading of the instructions is enough. Check them periodically; the directions sometimes change.

For mixing chemicals properly you need a good thermometer. Regular photographic thermometers are best, but a good baby bath thermometer will do. When you are ready to start mixing, fill a glass or enameled graduate, or a wide-mouthed jar with the amount of water at the temperature specified by the directions.

Don't dump water and chemicals into a bottle and shake like mad; use some sort of paddle or stirring rod. If overagitated, the solution will become mixed with air and may deteriorate quickly. Chemicals mix better when stirred. If the package contains a number of chemicals, make sure you dissolve them in the order called for in the instructions.

After the chemicals are completely dissolved, add colder water to make the required amount of solution, which can now be poured into a bottle for storing. Dark brown or opaque bottles make good containers, especially for developers. These chemicals are sensitive to light, as well as heat and humidity. If you keep your supplies in a dark cupboard, a clear glass bottle will serve just as well as the brown or opaque. Store supplies in a dark, cool, dry place. Keep all bottles tightly stoppered, after first filling them to capacity so that most of the air is excluded. Plastic bottles that are "squeezable" will allow you to force out the extra air before sealing. This prevents the contents from becoming exhausted by oxidation long before they should.

You can save a good portion of the money you spend on small quantities of paper developer, acid fixer, and some types of film developer by buying a large quantity and mixing up big batches. Eight one-pint bottles will hold one gallon of paper developer—by dividing the mixture up into small portions the containers will be full and the risk of oxidation reduced.

When buying film developer it is wise to pick up replenisher to go with it. You can make your developer go more than twice as far by adding the required amount of replenisher. Not only do you save money by making your original investment go farther, but you also insure your negatives against improper development by keeping your developer full strength.

Make sure you label your bottles, so you won't make the fatal mistake of trying to develop your films in the acid fixer. Masking tape or adhesive tape makes a good label. Even gummed paper labels can be used if they are covered with a clear plastic spray coating or shellac. This will attach the label permanently and render it waterproof. Spilled solutions or regular washing of the bottle will not cause the label to peel or discolor.

At the very beginning of your first efforts in the darkroom, try to teach yourself good darkroom habits. Keep your sinks and working surfaces clean at all times. After using the darkroom, wipe up all exposed surfaces that may have gotten wet. This not only makes for clean, neat appearance in your darkroom, but you'll find that it is safer to wipe up the excess liquid which happens to be splashed on the surroundings. This procedure also guards against unnecessary stains. Many photographic solutions will stain fabrics, woodwork, and porcelain unless washed off immediately.

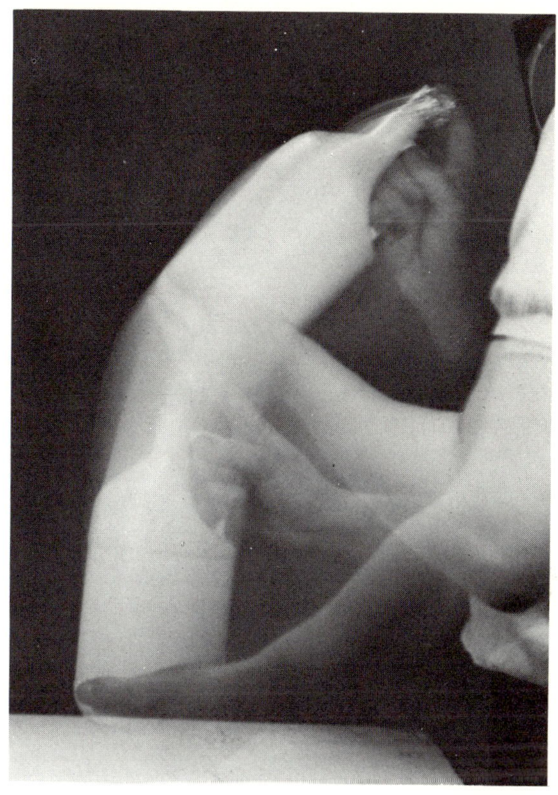

The Orientals have an expression about one picture being worth a thousand words. Well, the two pictures shown here are worth only one word between them—DON'T. The overenergetic technique of mixing chemicals shown at the right will only overaerate them and cause them to be partially exhausted before you even get to use them. And, the slap-dash method of filling a chemical tray shown below will fill the tray but at the risk of having the chemical splash over into neighboring trays. You need not move like a tortoise in your darkroom but considered deliberate activity is the best way to successful results.

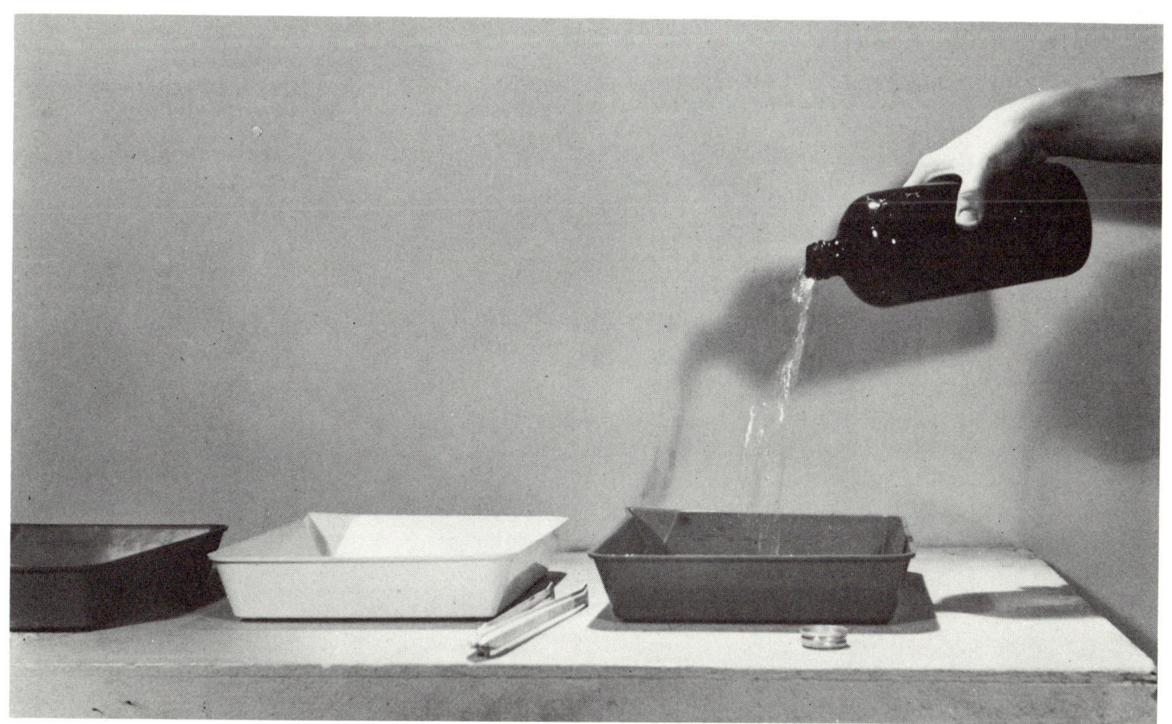

KEYS TO DARKROOM SUCCESS

1. The space you choose for your darkroom should be large enough, have conveniently placed electrical outlets (a must), and a water supply (a great plus, if possible). Lightproofing the area should be well figured out beforehand and carefully tested afterwards. Whatever materials you settle on for making your room lighttight—cardboards taped over windows, dark drapes, masking tape over door seams or lightleaking cracks—should be kept with your other darkroom supplies and reserved for this use only. Lightproofing should be made as much a matter of routine as possible— time spent looking for materials, or discovering some clever new way to rig things up is time stolen from your darkroom work.

2. Privacy is a must for successful darkroom work. This unfortunately rules out the bathroom as the working space in many family situations. Find a space that can be truly and exclusively yours for a few hours.

3. For your comfort, the room should be able to be ventilated. A linoleum flooring or a small washable mat under your feet will somewhat relieve the fatigue of standing. Include a stool or small chair if you have room for it.

4. Darkroom cleanliness is absolutely imperative. The floor, shelves, etc. should be washed down before use to eliminate dust and afterwards to remove any dumped or dripped chemicals.

5. Chemicals must be stored out of the reach of children and carefully segregated from each other. Beakers and mixing tools must be rinsed carefully after use.

6. Avoid such obvious conveniences as using a towel or the front of your apron to wipe your hands. You'll only wind up with dry hands and a chemically contaminated cloth ready to contaminate your hands on the next pass. Use paper towel instead and throw it away immediately after use.

7. Put up a reasonable supply of materials *plus* extra enlarger and safelight bulbs. All the processing and printing supplies in the world will not save the situation if one of your bulbs quits on you.

2

LOADING FILM

Most amateurs develop their films in what are known as "daylight" tanks using time and temperature methods. This chapter will discuss methods of loading various tanks and preparing the film for developing.

The most important piece of film developing equipment is the tank itself. Before buying a tank the beginner should consider his needs in relation to his darkroom facilities. Most tanks need to be loaded in complete darkness. If you lack facilities for light-tight working space, you must load your tank in a changing bag. The only other alternative is the use of a "daylight loading" tank for 35mm film only. These tanks are generally more complicated and expensive, but they allow the operator to load a roll of film in a lighted room.

Many developing tanks are made of plastic. Temperature is important in developing film and plastic tanks hold temperature well, insulating the contents from outside influences. Stainless steel tanks are generally standard for the more advanced darkroom worker. These tanks quickly transmit any changes in outside temperature. This allows the worker to maintain desired developer temperature by placing the tank in a tray of water to form a water jacket. By controlling the temperature of the water in the tray, you also control the temperature of the developer in the tank.

When buying a developing tank you must also consider some other points. Do you need an adjustable tank, or one that takes a specific size? Does the lid lock securely in place? Is it easy to agitate? Does it require an excessive amount of solution? Is it easy to load? Selection is a matter of personal choice so take your pick after considering all these features.

The main idea in loading a developing tank is to remove the exposed film from its light-tight container and thread the length of the film into spiral grooves in the two flanges of the tank reel.

There are two main types of tanks designed for loading in the dark: those that require winding the film on the reel from the inside out, and those that wind from the outside in. The latter uses a semi-automatic loading principle in which the two sides of the reel are alternately twisted back and forth and the film is gripped and moved ahead slightly with each cycle. The channel is long enough to accommodate two rolls of 120 or 620 film if the film is loaded with care, but it will take only one roll of 35mm. Other makes of outside-in winders are manually operated and as easily loaded.

Loading film into reels in the dark is a task that creates problems for some workers, yet the solution is rather simple. It just takes practice and patience. An easy way to practice is to use a roll of outdated film. Open the roll and try loading it in the light, with your eyes open until you familiarize yourself with the procedure. You will be able to see your mistakes and you can correct them as you learn. After you have tried it a few times, try it with your eyes closed to get the feel of doing it in the dark. Then take a look at your efforts. After a while you will begin to get the hang of it. If you don't have a roll of old film handy to use for practice, ask your camera shop if they have a roll or two of old film lying around. This practice will take a little time, but it will pay off when you begin to handle your exposed film.

Plastic film aprons are also available for use in film processing. These resemble nothing so much as they do a plastic lasagna noodle. They are long plastic strips with crimped edges and one end rolled back on itself and held in place with a rivet. The square-cut end of the film is tucked into the turned back end and the film and apron are rolled up together. Using aprons requires far less dexterity than using reels.

After loading the exposed film onto the reel or apron place it inside the tank. Be sure the lid fits tight. You are now ready to complete the operation of processing your film with the lights on.

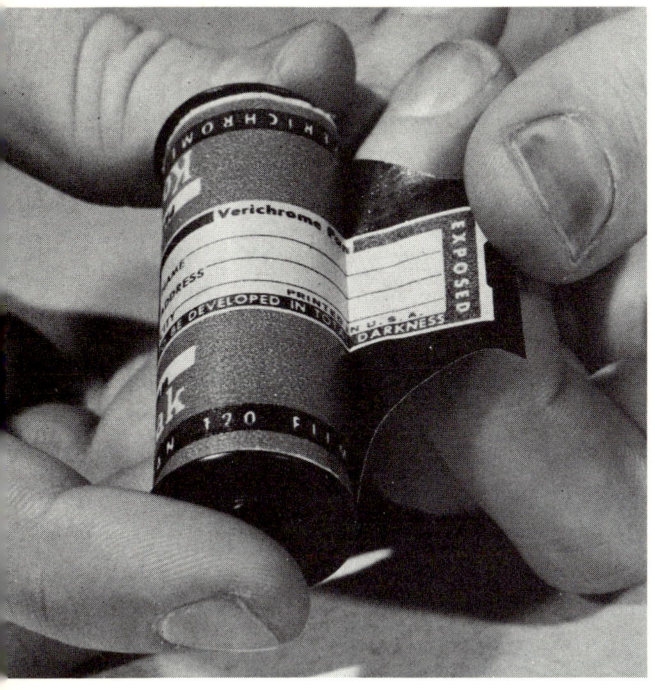

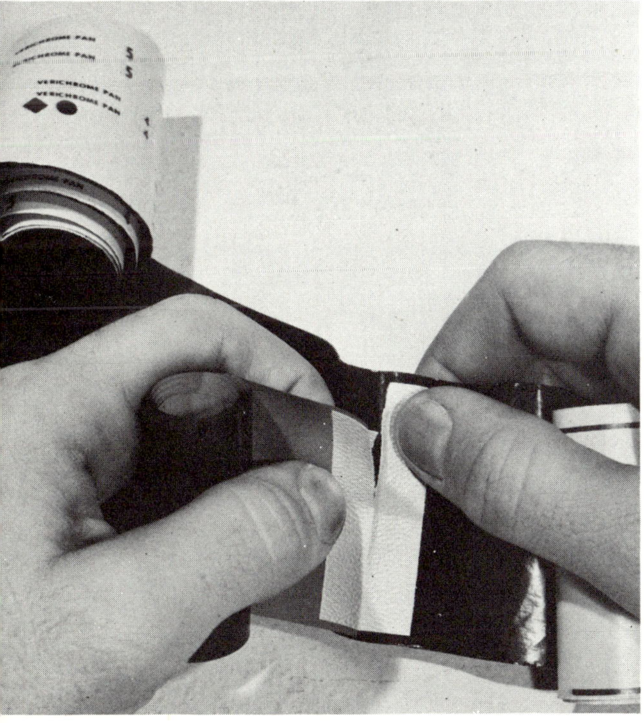

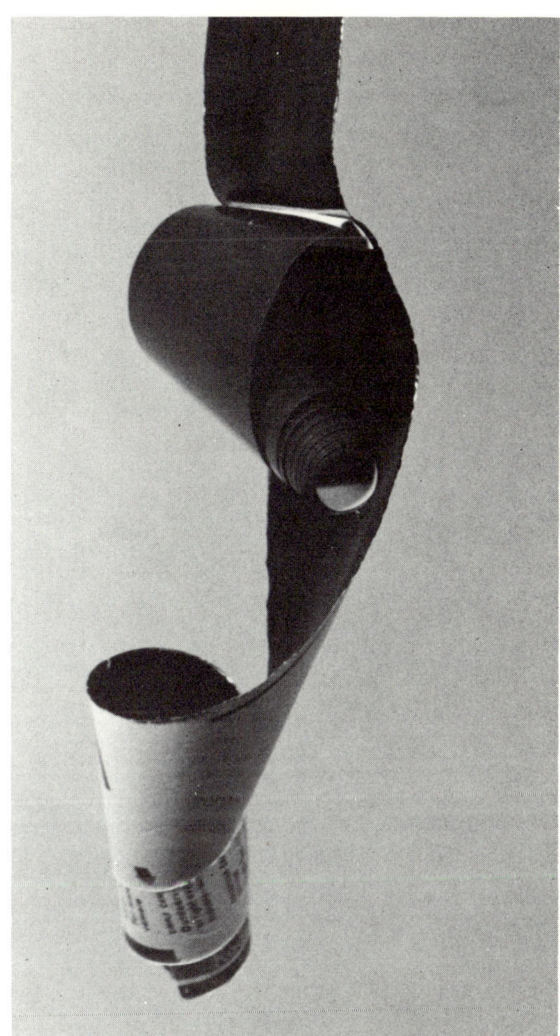

120 and 220 films come wrapped on a metal spool with a protective paper wrapper. To begin loading, the seal is broken in total darkness—either in the darkroom or within a changing bag. The film is unrolled and the inside end is removed from the spool. Then the paper backing is removed from the film. Be careful to keep your fingers off the film at all times, handling it only by the edges.

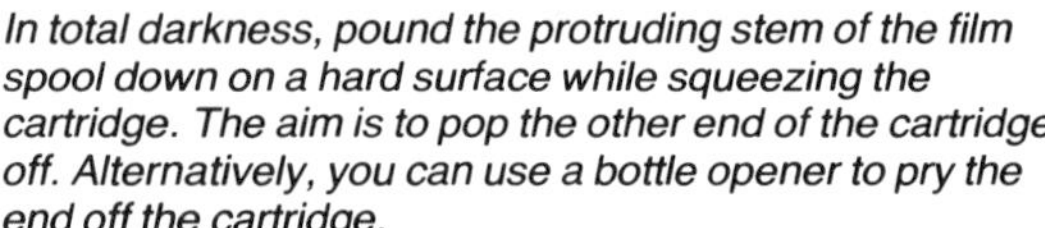

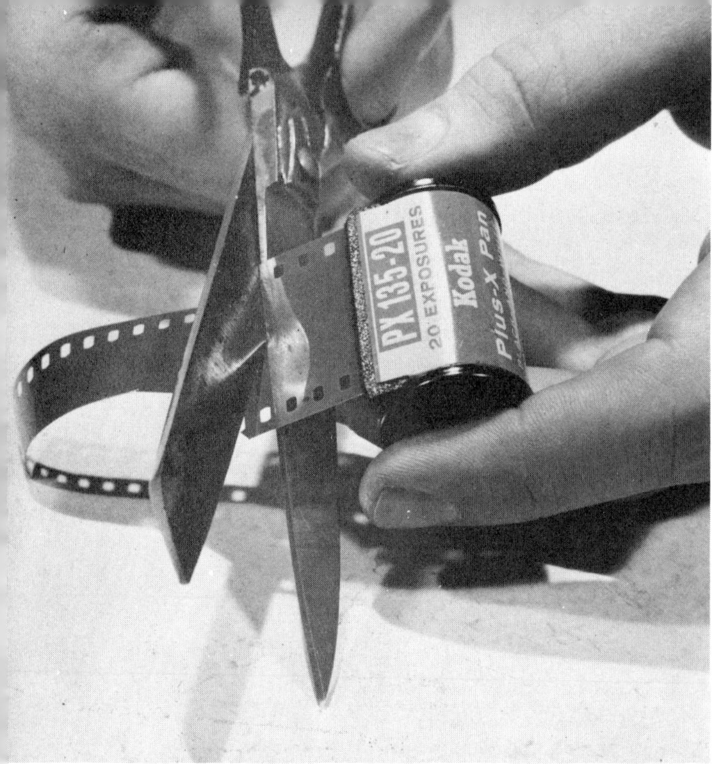

If you have left the film leader out when you rewound your 35mm film into its cartridge, the first loading step is to trim it off.

In total darkness, pound the protruding stem of the film spool down on a hard surface while squeezing the cartridge. The aim is to pop the other end of the cartridge off. Alternatively, you can use a bottle opener to pry the end off the cartridge.

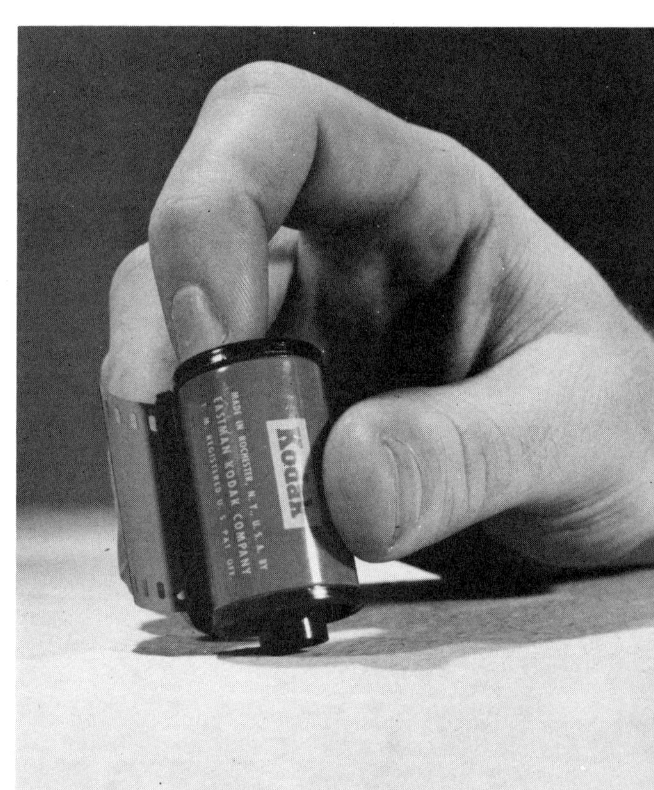

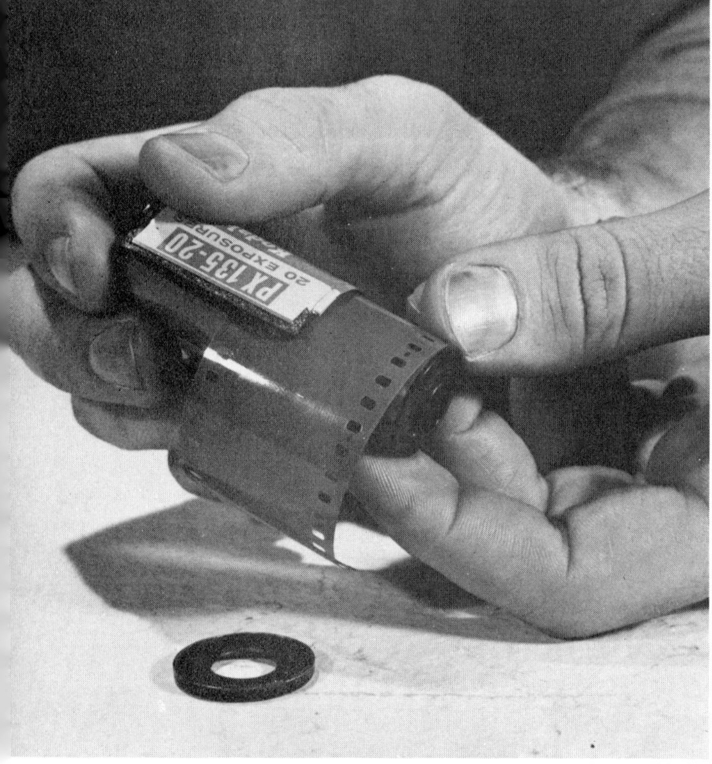

Once the cartridge end is removed, you can drop out the film on its spool. If the leader has not yet been cut off, do so now.

The inside end of the film is taped to the spool. Cut it free as close to the spool as possible.

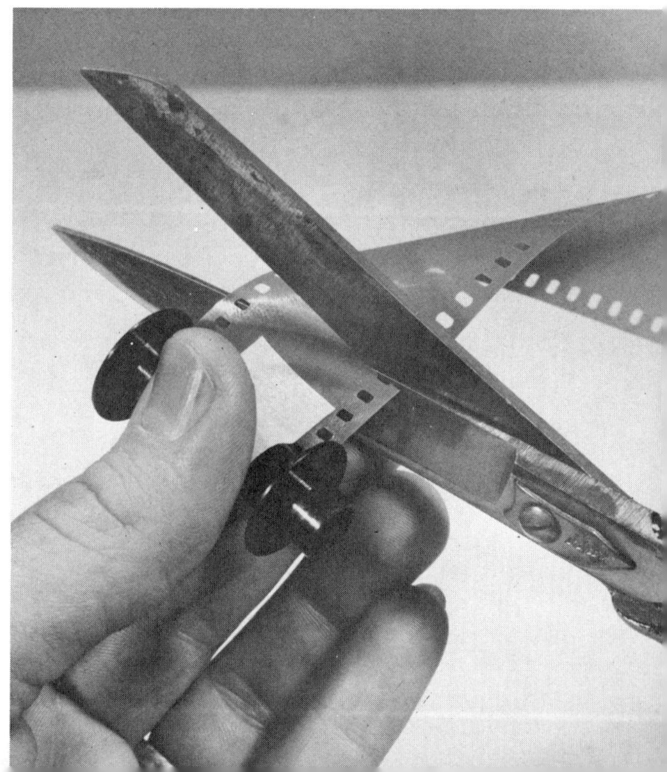

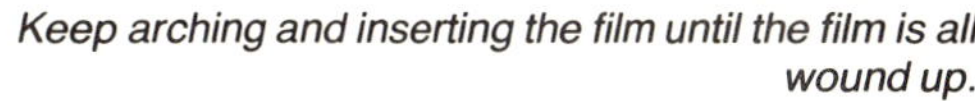

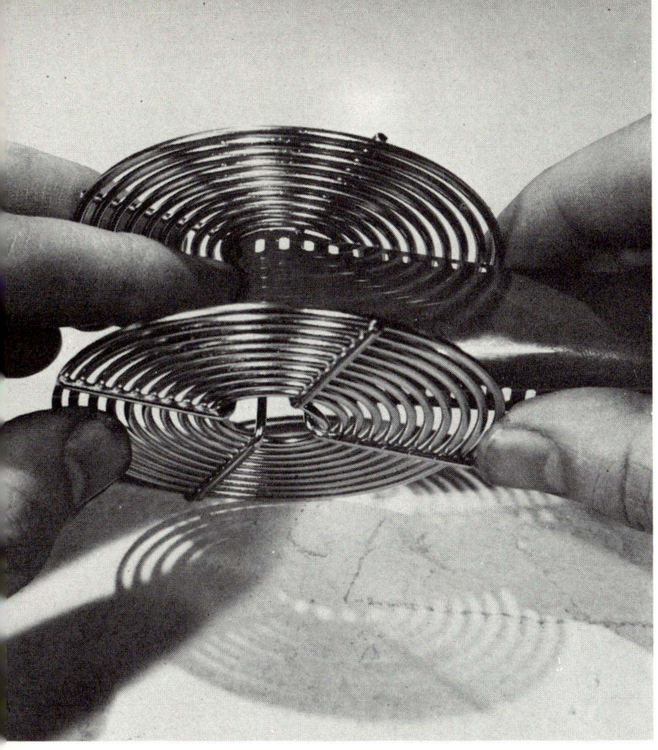

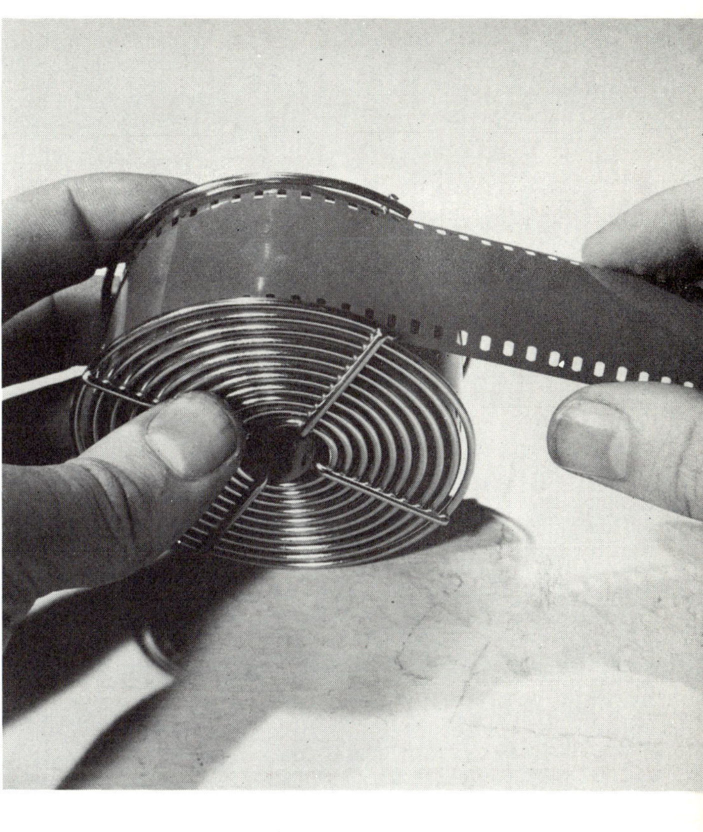

Begin inserting the film onto the reel. Some reels feature a film clip in the center that makes it easier to get it started. Notice that with the stainless steel reel shown, it is necessary to arch the film slightly to fit it into the reel.

A daylight-loading tank such as that shown below allows for loading film in normal room light. When the film is rewound, the leader must be left protruding. Then, the exposed film is placed in the smaller chamber with the leader passing into the larger chamber. The film is then drawn into the larger chamber for processing.

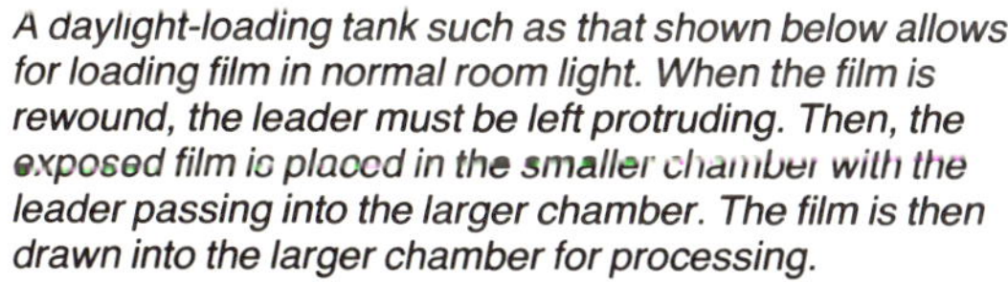

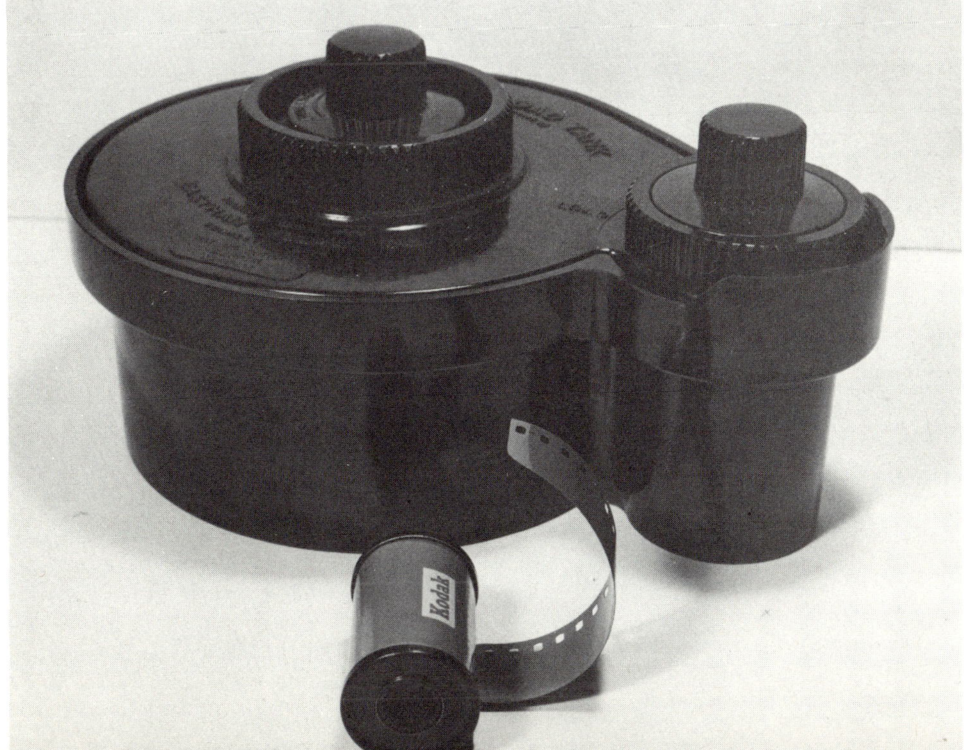

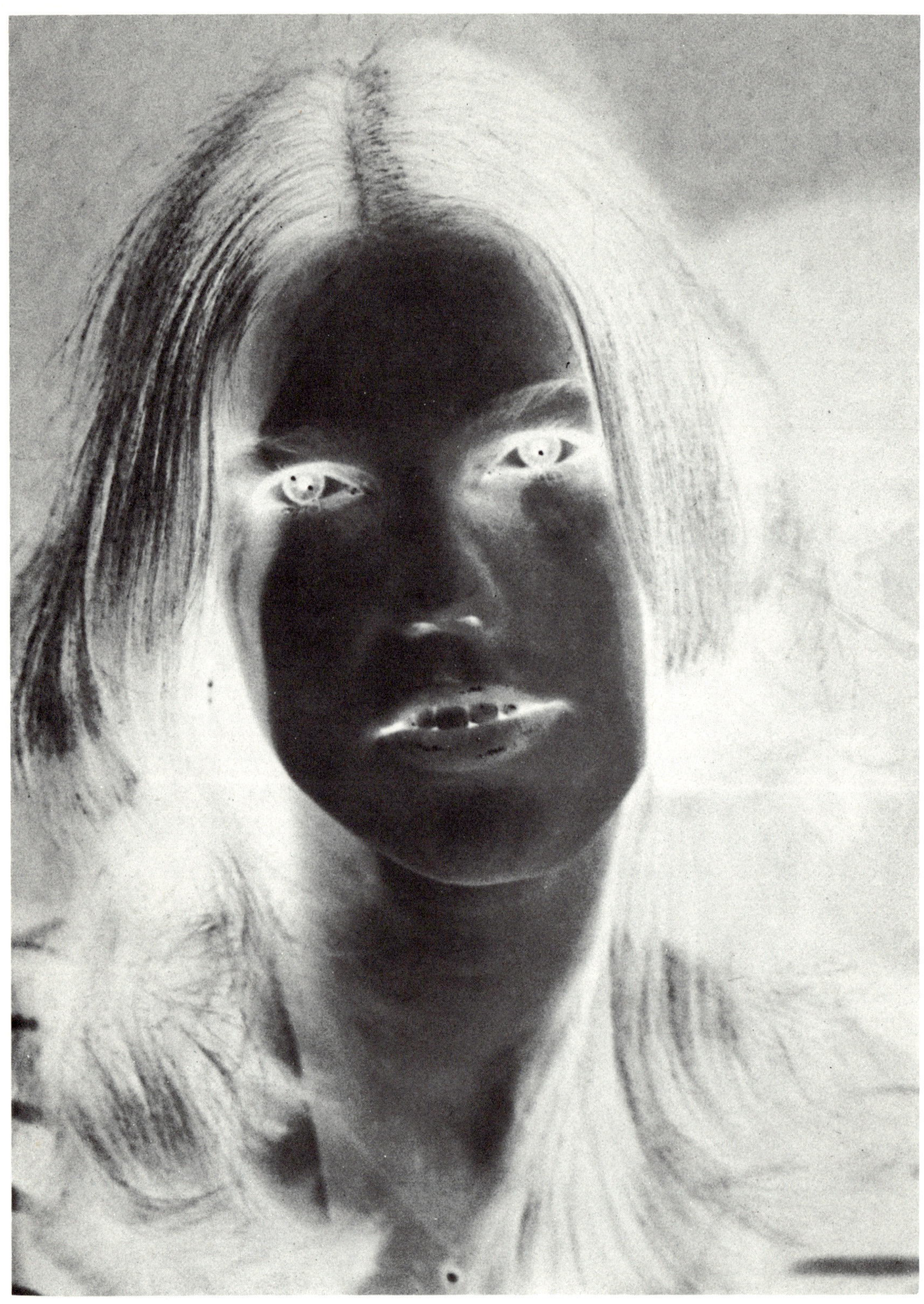

A well-developed negative is the first step toward a fine result. For optimum results, be sure to follow manufacturers' directions for both film and chemicals.

DEVELOPING FILM

Film developing is basically a very simple process that anyone can perform with a minimum of darkroom equipment and supplies. It consists of immersing the film into a developer solution long enough for the chemical process to take place. Then it is necessary to put the film through an acid fixer to wash away all undeveloped silver and to harden the emulsion of the film to make it last.

As explained previously, the film emulsion is sensitive to light and has to be handled in complete darkness. With "daylight" tanks, there is no need for a special darkened room for film developing, other than the darkness required for loading the film into the tank. The tank cannot be opened to the light until the film has been completely developed and fixed, but there are provisions on the lids of all makes of tanks for pouring chemicals in and out, without letting in light.

Developing times are given by developer manufacturers as well as in the instructions packed with most films. Be sure to read and follow instructions carefully. These times have been computed after careful testing and study. With correct exposures, you should get normal negatives. It is possible to time the development of films by using a watch or clock, but if you do much work you will find a timer made for the purpose more convenient. You can set the timer for any duration and as the time passes you will always know how much time is left. At the end of this period of time, there will be a very audible buzz or bell. This automatic timer gives you freedom and makes it easier for you to develop film without continually concentrating directly on watching the clock.

Another important factor in developing film is temperature. This is also dictated by the manufacturer. Before pouring the developer into the tank check the temperature of the solution. This should be about 68° F. If the solution is too cool or too warm it should be warmed or cooled till it reaches the right temperature. Don't try diluting the developer with water. This will weaken it and make it undependable. The simplest method is to stand the jar or bottle of developer in a tray of water. The temperature of the water around the bottle can be adjusted up or down as desired. When the developer reaches the right temperature, you can proceed with development.

Don't forget to check the temperature of the fixer. It should vary no more than three degrees either way from the temperature of the developer.

Be sure to check the temperature of your rinse water also. Even normal tap water could be too hot in summer, too cold in winter. For best results the rinse should be within three degrees of the developer temperature. If you have a mixer faucet you can probably mix hot and cold water to reach the correct degree. If you have separate hot and cold taps, you will probably have to run the amount of hot or cold water needed to bring the water to the correct temperature into containers.

Plastic developing tanks will usually hold the temperature of the solution placed in the tank for the duration of the developing time. Outside temperature does not affect this type of tank very quickly. On the other hand the stainless steel tank changes very quickly to adjust to the temperature of its surroundings. It is usually best to place a steel tank in temperature-controlled water throughout the developing process to hold it to the correct temperature. It is removed only to agitate at the prescribed intervals. Of course, if your room temperature is not far from the desired temperature, the temperature of the solution in the tank will not be affected in the short time in the developer.

After you have mastered the developing steps, by developing several rolls of film, it is best to standardize your processing routine. Pick one developer and one fixer (commonly called hypo) that works for you, and stick with it. This will simplify matters, cutting down on storage space needed and making less chance for mixup in using the wrong time or temperature for other solutions.

One other item of importance is to agitate

properly during development to assure that fresh developer reaches all the areas of the film. The correct method is to agitate at regular intervals. This gives time for the chemical action to take place while the tank is motionless. Then when you agitate, you move the developer around, moving fresh developer to replace that which has been exhausted. Over-agitation will make the film develop unevenly.

The life of your film developer can be extended greatly by using replenisher. This assures you of a standardized solution for even developing action, even over a long period of time. It also saves money, by letting you continue to use a solution that would otherwise be discarded. Replenisher is added to the developer bottle in specified amounts for each roll of film developed. This is usually one ounce for each roll. Add replenisher to the developer bottle before pouring back the used solution, and discard the small amount of used developer left over. This replenishment makes the developer as good as new, even though with use it sometimes will become cloudy and dirty looking. This is normal and does not affect the action of the chemicals.

Hypo should be changed periodically, since it loses its effectiveness with use. The more it is used, the more time it takes to do the same job that it did when fresh. Manufacturer's instructions will usually give times for the fixer bath for a fresh solution and the added amount of time it takes as it gets older, along with the approximate number of rolls of film it will process. After extended use, hypo will become completely exhausted and should be discarded. It is best to use a chemical test to be sure whether it is still good or not. This is described in more detail in the chapter on handling chemicals. (Many photographers do not reuse hypo at all.)

After you have finished the developing and fixing process you will have negatives from which, as soon as the negatives have been washed and dried, you can make prints. Your negative is considered normal if it displays a wide range of separated tones, from the highlights to the shadows, with all of the grays in between. This is the type of negative that should print on a normal, or #2, grade of printing paper. After some experience you will be able to judge the density of your negatives, even before making prints, to determine if your negatives are under- or overexposed or otherwise need improvement.

The photographer who uses a changing light source for viewing negatives will never be able to judge his developed negatives correctly. He may judge his negatives by a darkroom safelight, a retouching desk, light reflected from a work table, or even by holding the negative up directly to a bare light bulb. Any of these methods is sufficient if the method is always kept standard.

One of the many types of negatives and transparency viewers is best for this purpose, but if you do not have one, be sure to standardize your procedure. If you are using an adjustable light source, be sure that the intensity of the viewing light is always kept constant. If you are using a card and reflected light, make sure the distance between the light source and the card is always the same, so that the intensity will always be constant. Only under controlled lighting and viewing conditions will you be able to judge negative quality correctly and decide on corrective or creative techniques for the future.

When film has been thoroughly fixed it should be transferred to the wash water and agitated well for a few seconds. As soon as the tank fills with water, dump it and refill. This eliminates most of the fixer on the surfaces of the film and further washing will take it out of the emulsion and replace it with water. In washing film it is very important that it is not in surface contact with something else. The water must have free access to all parts of the film surface to obtain efficient washing.

To reduce the film washing time, you can use one of the many "hypo eliminators" on the market. After rinsing your film briefly, soak it in a dilute solution of the eliminator. Be sure to follow the manufacturer's recommendations as to the dilution and the length of soaking time (usually about two minutes). After that, it is only necessary to wash the film for an abbreviated time.

After the film has been washed, it should be immersed in a wetting agent before being hung up to dry; however, with some types of water this is not sufficient to give you clean negatives. If your water supply has a tendency to leave a scum on the negatives, they must be wiped with cotton or a clean sponge to remove this scum before drying. If the scum is allowed to dry on the negative, it is difficult to remove, if not impossible. In this case the water is at fault rather than your processing technique, but it still must be corrected.

Hanging film to dry is a relatively simple operation. Film clips are available for hanging film, but most every household has the ordinary wooden clothespin, which is cheaper and does the job just as well. After the film has been hung to dry it should not be disturbed until completely dry. If it is taken down with the edges still wet, it is very easy to cause a drop of water to move across the surface of the negative in an area where it is already dry. When this happens, it can cause a streak that cannot be removed. Drying may be done at ordinary room temperature, or it can be speeded up slightly by using a fan to cause a movement of air around the film. If you are in a hurry for the film to dry, you can use heated air to speed up the process considerably. Drying conditions should not be changed, though, in the middle of the drying period, for this can cause a type of water spotting or streaking.

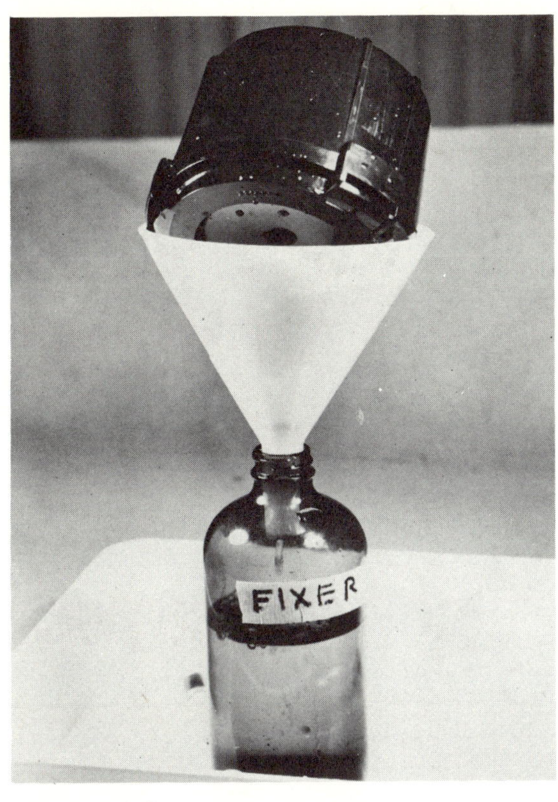

Proper film washing must remove all traces of chemicals from your film. The first step is to drain all the fixer from the tank as shown at left. Then, remove the lid and fill the tank with water. Make sure first that the water is neither too hot nor too cold. When the tank is filled, you can set it down under the faucet to continue washing for about 30 minutes. The washed film should be hung to dry in a dust free place.

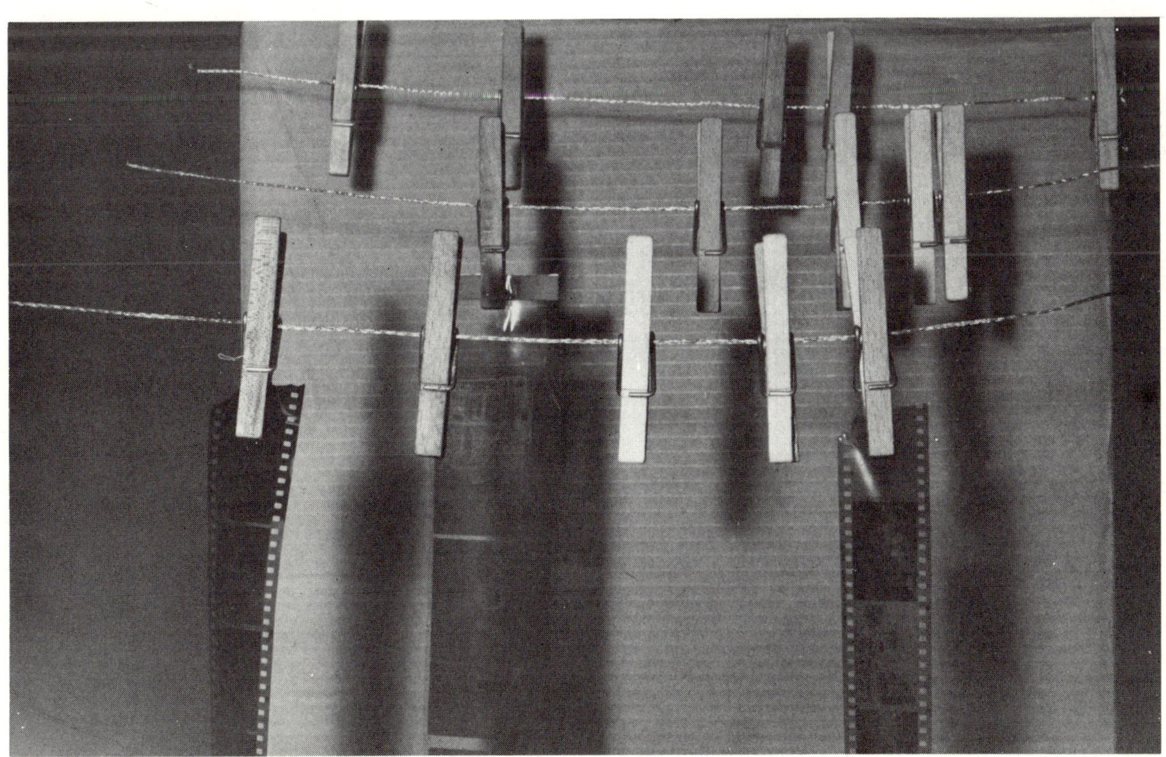

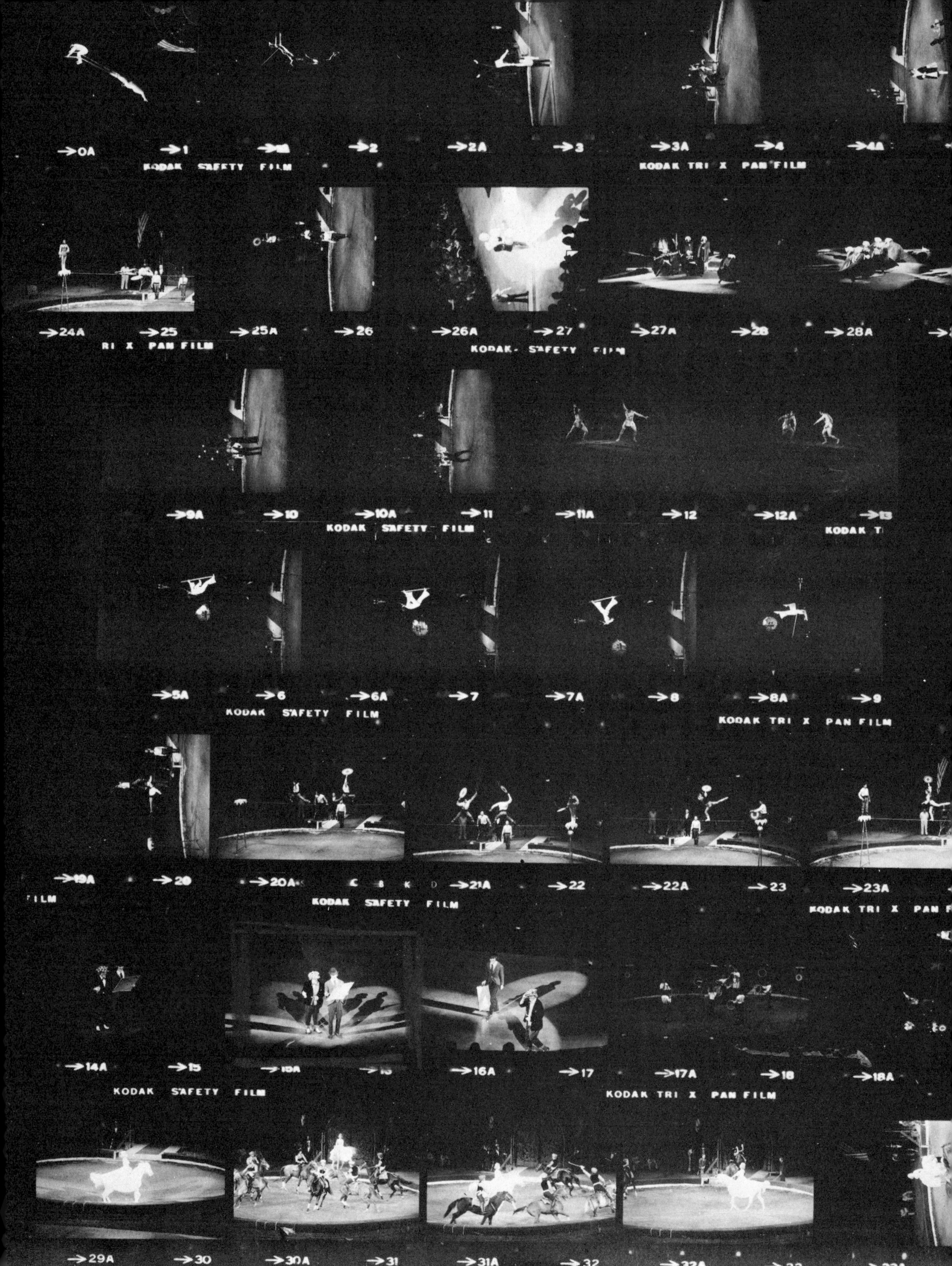

CONTACT PRINTING

CONTACT PRINTING

It is a good idea to make contact prints of every picture you shoot—as a permanent record and an aid to choosing the negatives you want to enlarge. By far the easiest and quickest method of making contact prints is to print a full roll at a time, using 8″ × 10″ enlarging paper, a sheet of glass taped to a good stiff cardboard along one edge, and a bare light bulb or your enlarger as a light source. If you work carefully you can get high quality results.

Contact prints are the best way of testing a negative, as well as determining the most suitable paper on which to make enlargements. Since #2 paper is normal, it is a good choice for a beginning. If it gives you a normal print—that is, a print with a good range of tones—you have a normal negative. If the contact print on #2 shows up too soft, then #3, the next higher degree of contrast, should be used for the enlargements. If the contact print on #2 is too hard a print, or too contrasty, try #1.

Contact prints can be made on a flat table with a printing light overhead about three feet away. A 60-watt bulb is strong enough, but you can compensate for a stronger lamp by shortening the exposure.

If you use the enlarger as your light source, set up the darkroom as if you were going to make enlargements. Raise the enlarger until the light covers the baseboard.

With the lights off, you now handle the paper and do the developing by the light of a safelight. Be sure the safelight is suitable for the paper you are using. Place the paper on the cardboard with the emulsion side up.

Now place your strips of negatives, emulsion (dull) side down on the paper. One 8″ × 10″ sheet will hold a full roll of 120 film if it is cut into strips of four frames each, or a roll of 35mm film. (Always remember the paper and film should be placed emulsion to emulsion.) Finally, close the tape-hinged glass down over the paper and negatives.

To make the exposure, you simply turn on the enlarger light or overhead bulb. Only experience can give you any exposure hints as negatives differ in strength and require different exposures. The light source will also vary.

If your roll of film contains negatives of varying densities that will require different exposures, you can give different exposures to the various negatives by cutting pieces of cardboard to cover the ones needing less exposure. First, an overall exposure is given, based on the less dense negatives. Then all except the denser frames are covered with the cardboard and given additional exposure as needed. These exposure times can only be determined by tests. Eventually you will learn the approximate exposure needed for your average negatives.

The same principle of printing applies to using a commercially available printing frame, except that the negative and glass are held tightly in place by the spring back of the frame.

The most elaborate way of making contact prints is to use the contact printer. It consists of a box containing one or more white light bulbs, along with a red bulb which is used for viewing and setting the negative in place to print. On top is a sheet of glass on which you place the negative, and a pressure device to hold the negative and paper firmly in contact during exposure. An important feature of the contact printer is the built-in switch for exposing the paper. All you do is press the switch for the amount of time you think will be right for printing each particular negative. This time can only be determined by trial and error. Make sure you are using contact printing paper; enlarging paper won't work in the contact printer.

Once your prints have been developed and dried, you can study them. By making a print of each negative you can more easily select the best negatives in a roll and concentrate on making good finished prints of a few choice negatives. These decisions very easily give you a solid basis for planning an enlarging session. Choose a reasonable quantity of work, isolate the corresponding negatives, and get to work.

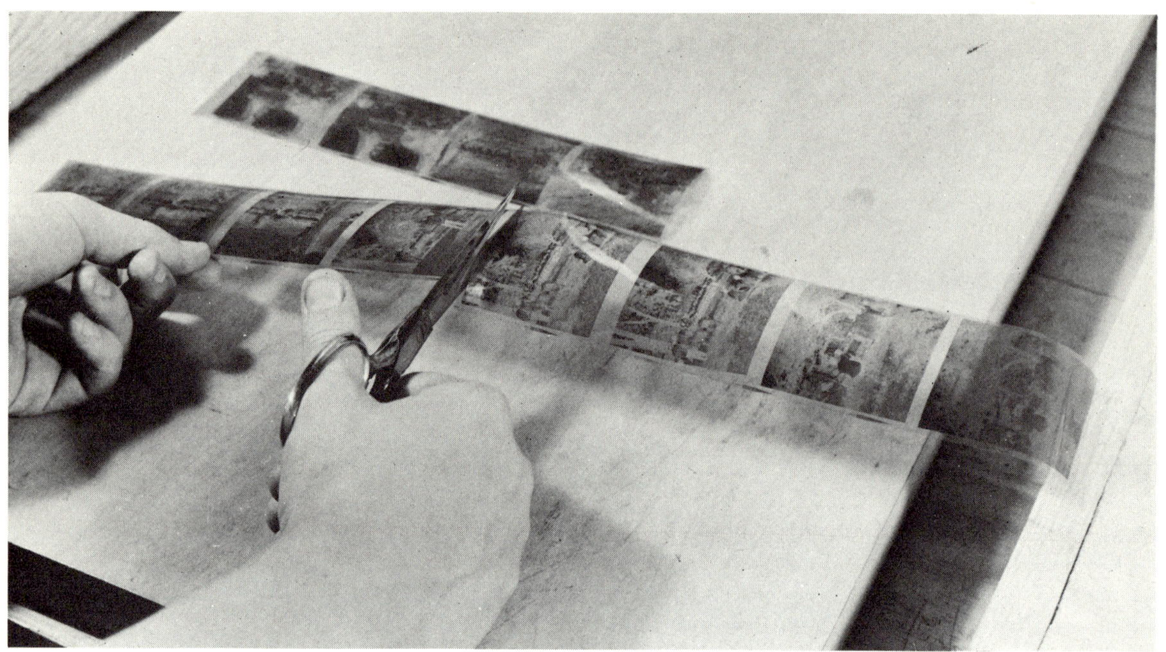

The first step in making a contact sheet is cutting the negatives into strips that will fit on your paper (above). Next, the negative strips are laid on the paper with the emulsion side down (below). Then a glass is laid over the paper and negatives to hold them flat (opposite top) and the exposure is made. The finished contact sheet should be examined with a magnifying glass as shown to choose those frames you wish to enlarge.

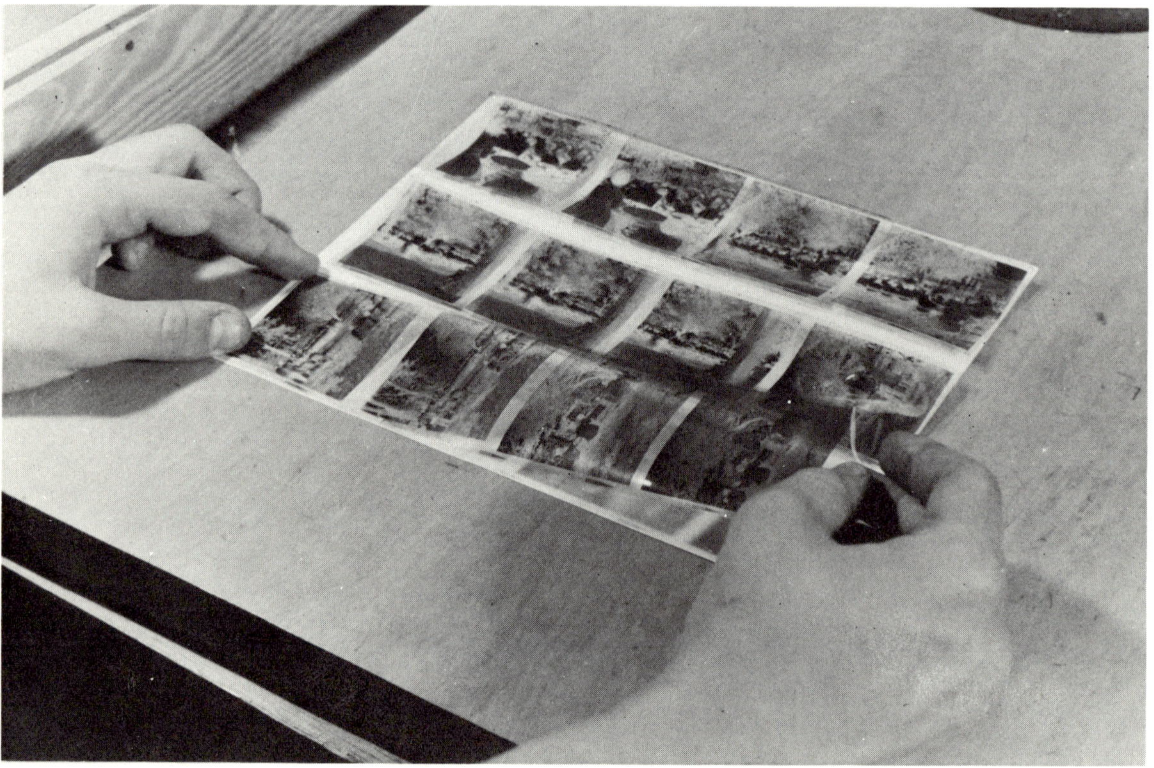

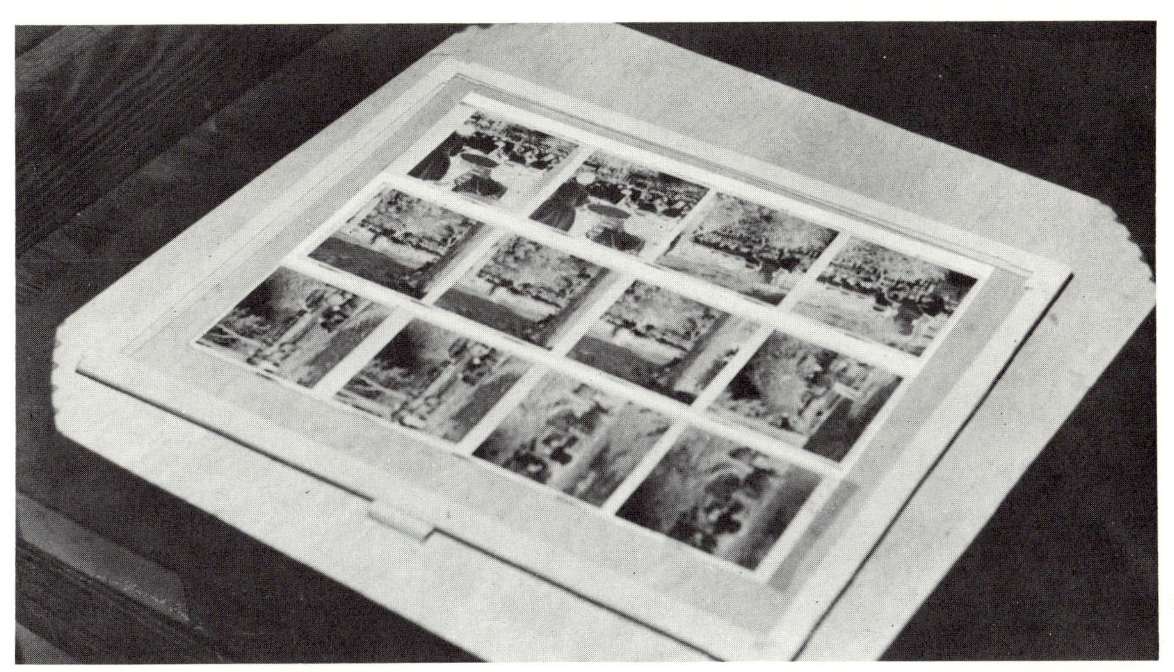

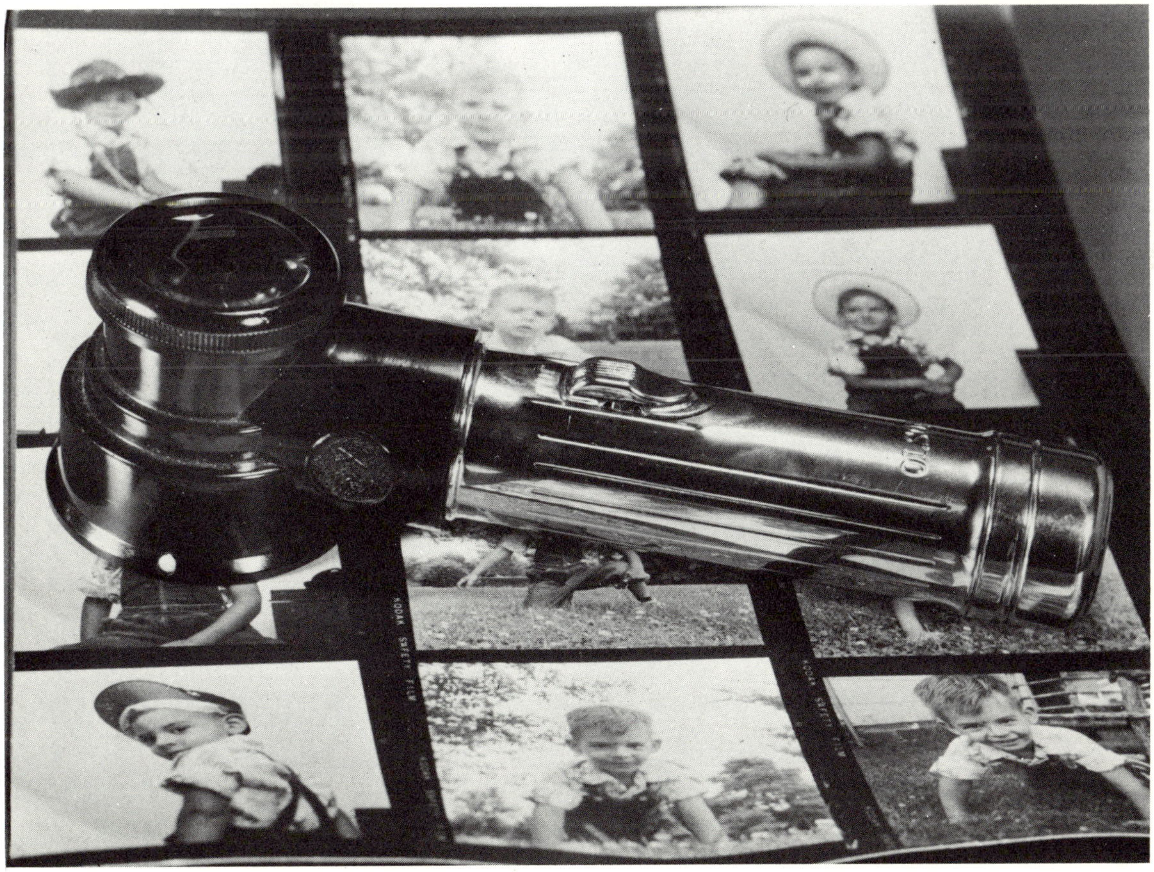

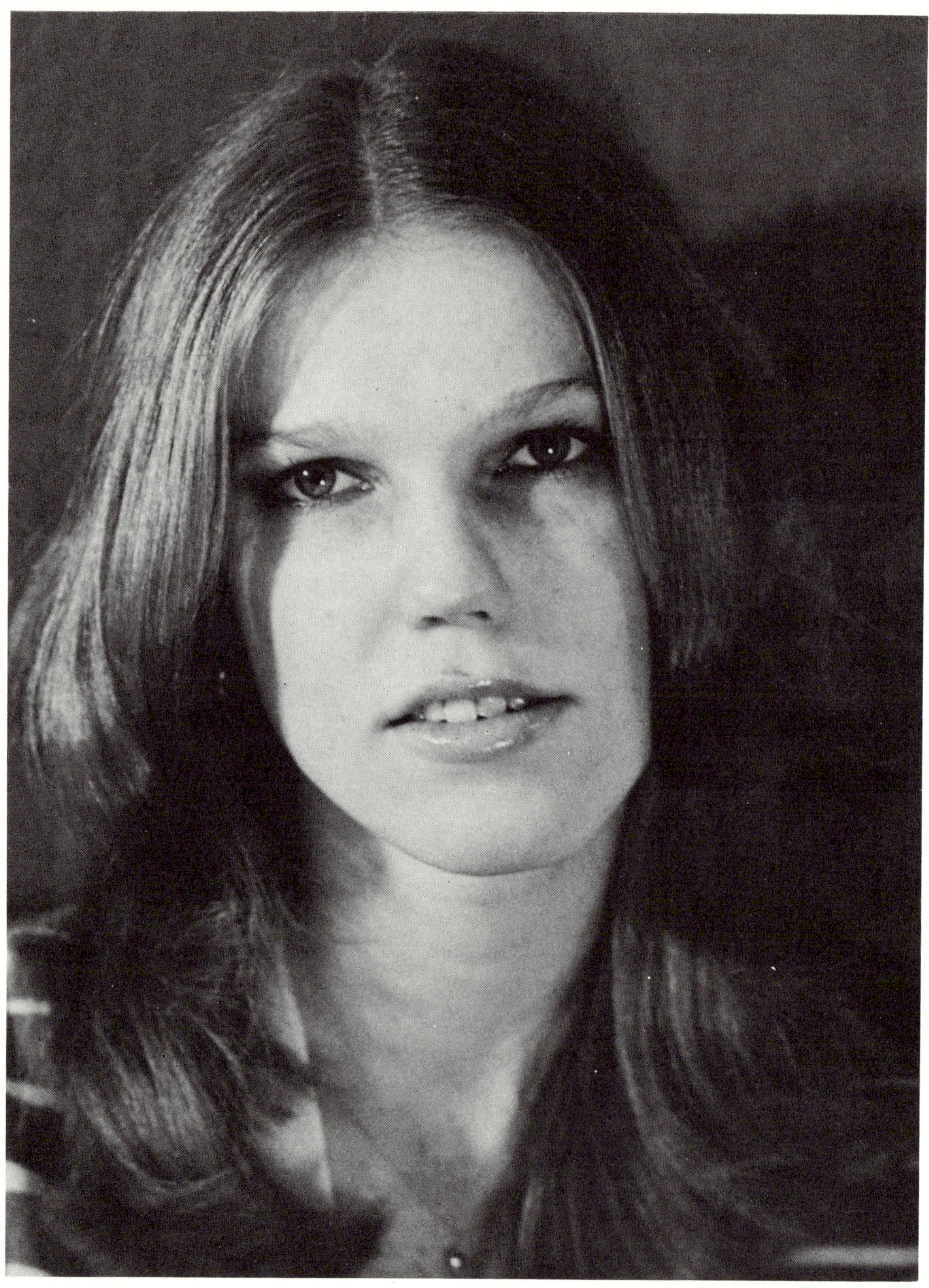

Making an enlargement is one of the most exciting moments of darkroom work. This is the point at which you really see your efforts pay off.

ENLARGING FUNDAMENTALS

The series of pictures of the little girl with the big hat reproduced here shows what can be done with the enlarger. The contact print shows what a picture looks like when printed the same size as the negative. The larger prints show what enlargements look like—first, when all of the negative is included, then at varying degrees of cropping. The beginner is usually rather timid about enlarging since he has been used to the common "drugstore prints," but with a little experimenting he can learn that it pays to explore his negatives. Sometimes a print can be improved by cropping out distracting backgrounds or making an extreme enlargement. It's quite a thrill to watch a good picture that you have created from an ordinary negative "come up" in the developer tray.

Many different makes of enlargers are on the market, all with their own particular features. The modern photographer is often not too interested in the mechanics of enlarger construction, yet it is good to have a basic idea of what the enlarger does. Basically, the enlarger projects the negative image onto paper. The paper on which the enlarged negative image is projected is exposed to light and developed, fixed, and washed to make a print.

Degree of enlargement is controlled by the up and down movement of the enlarger head. The lower it is (closer to the baseboard), the smaller the image will be. As the enlarger head is raised on the supporting post, the image gets correspondingly larger. You are limited only by the capabilities of your enlarger and the quality of your negative.

The projected image is focused optically by turning a knob which moves the lens closer or father away from the negative. Some enlarger models feature ease of operation with automatic focusing of the image as the enlarger head is moved up or down.

THE ENLARGER

The enlarger is probably the piece of darkroom equipment for which you will spend the major share of your budget. You should choose in reference to both the present and future. The Durst F-60 enlarger shown at right allows for printing both 35mm and 2¼" x 2¼" negatives and for color printing. It is a little more expensive than smaller models that allow only for 35mm printing but its versatility makes it well worth its price. A second feature that should be considered is storage. This model is easily disassembled —the baseboard, column, and head come apart for easy storage.

Parts:
A. Enlarger head
B. Fine-focusing knob
C. Lens with adjustable diaphragm ring
D. Knob for vertical movement of head
E. Column
F. Baseboard

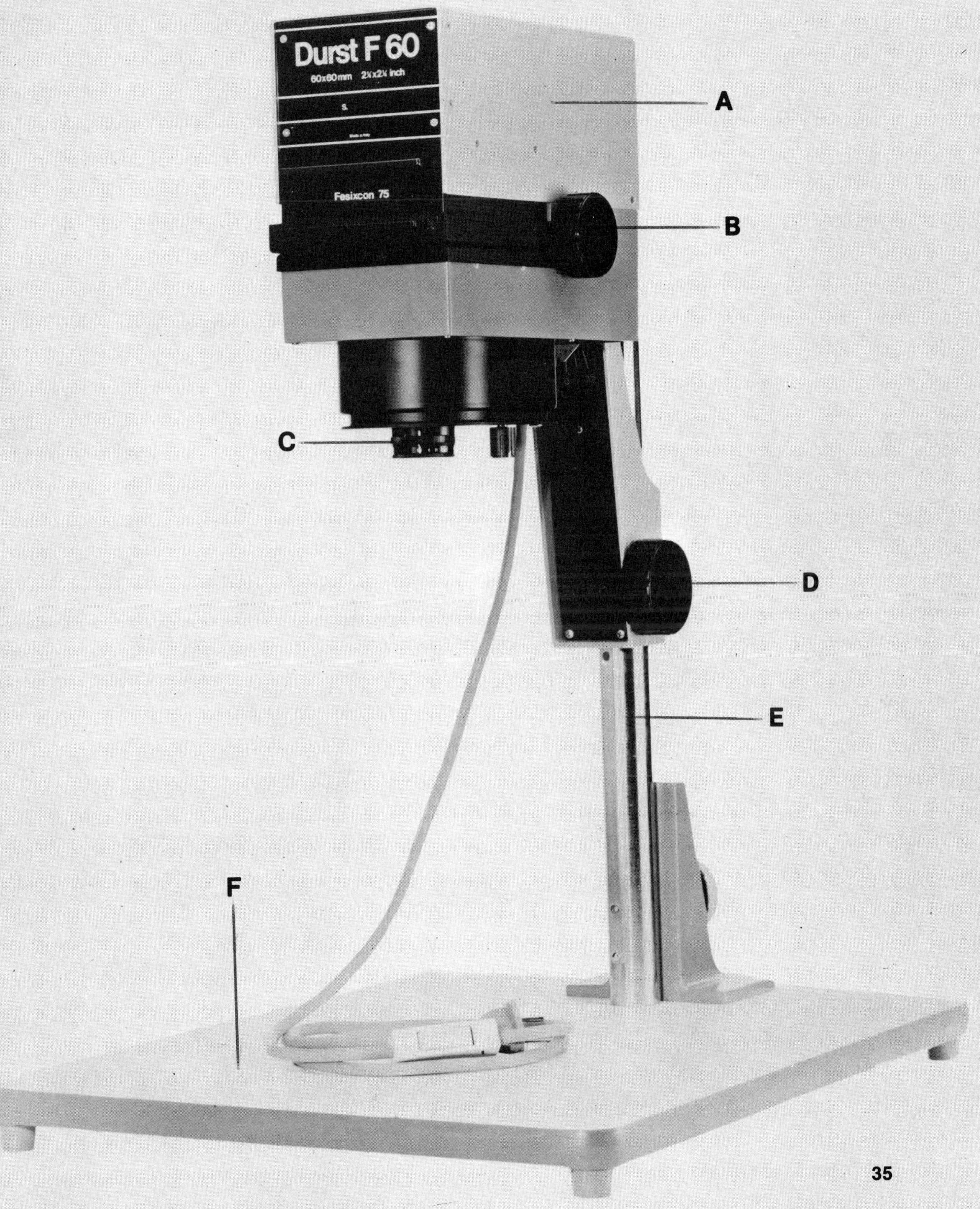

Durst F 60
60x60mm 2¼x2¼ inch
Fesixcon 75
A
B
C
D
E
F

Enlarging your own pictures makes it possible to create new croppings in the darkroom. The sequence of prints shown on these pages demonstrates the possibilities of a single negative. A contact print of the entire negative is shown at the right. Below are two tighter croppings. Opposite, the mid-range portrait has been transformed into a tight head shot.

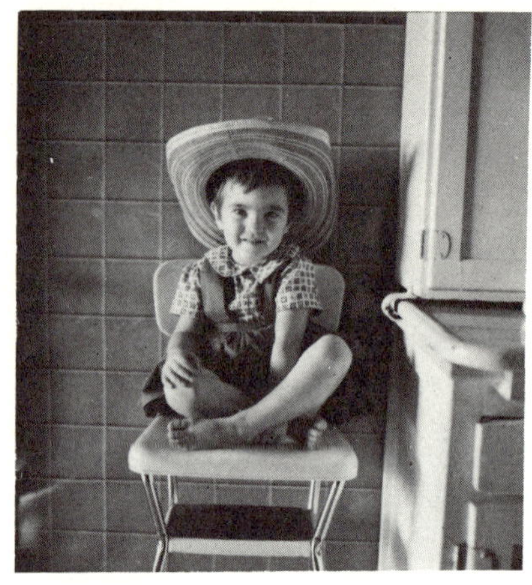

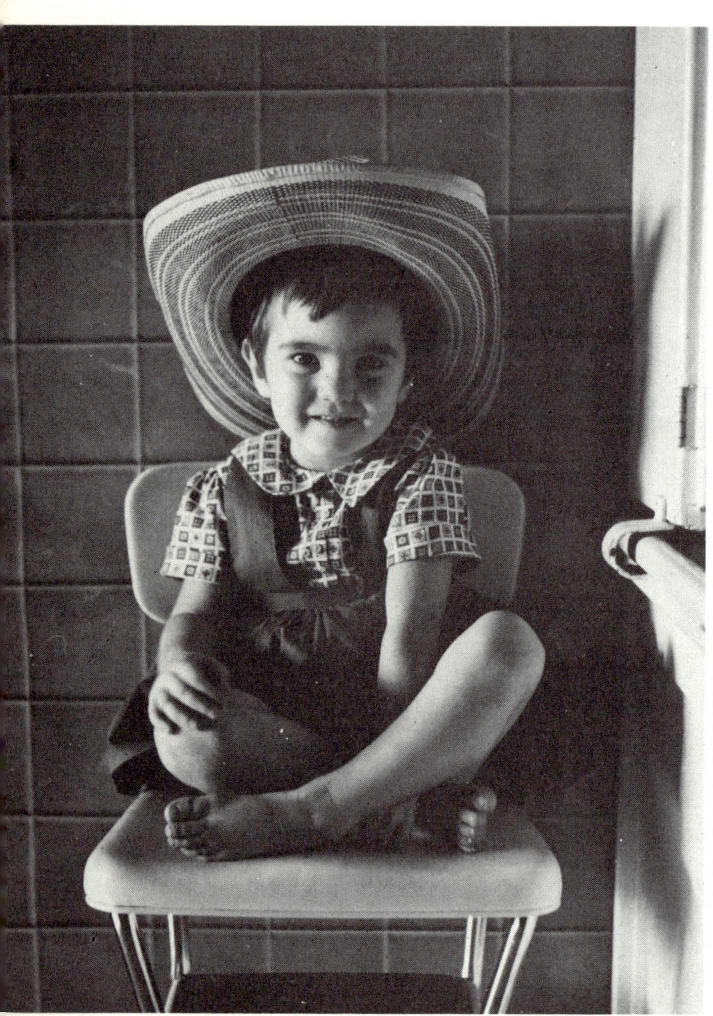

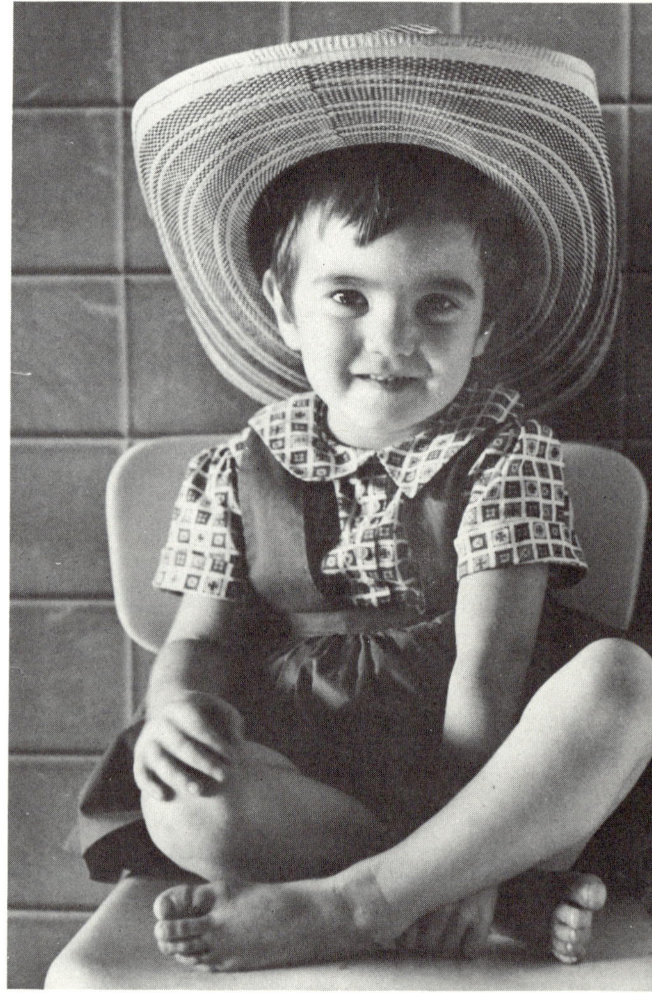

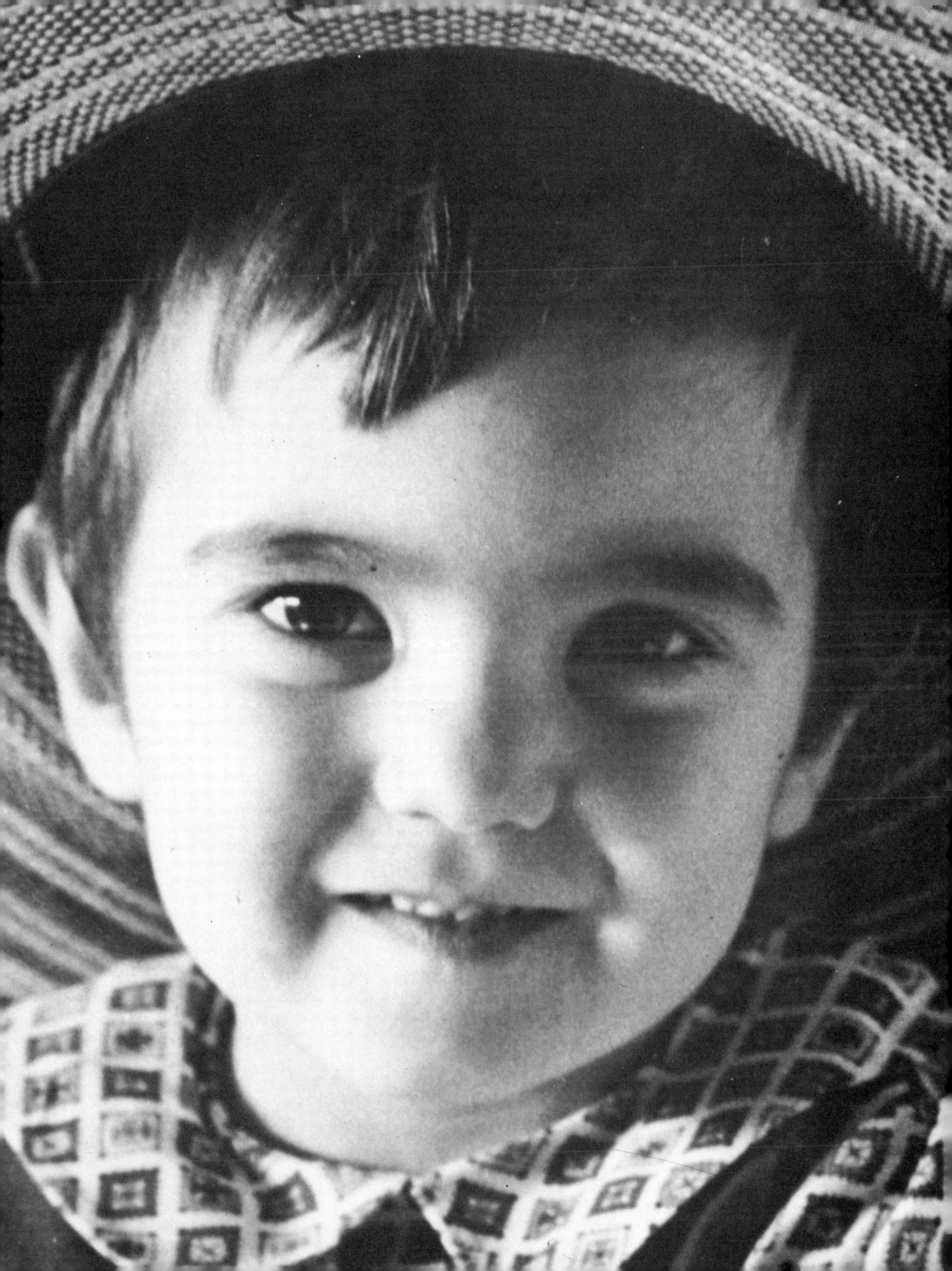

MAKING THE ENLARGEMENT

Enlarging the photograph is done by placing the negative in an enlarger which projects the image vertically onto a baseboard under the enlarger.

It is necessary to have some sort of easel to hold the printing paper flat. Many types are available. Some are adjustable, with movable arms that can be set for different size prints. Others are made to accommodate prints in four different standard sizes. These easels are set to make a 1/4-inch border on all prints. Other methods of holding the paper can be adapted when borderless prints are desired.

Enlarging exposure times can be reckoned by counting, by watching the clock, or by using various types of automatic timers. Counting of exposure time is not reliable because it will vary from one time to the next and can be inaccurate. Experienced operators can count seconds with surprising accuracy, once they have learned to maintain a precise cadence, but it is preferable to have a clock close by that ticks loudly to help control the tempo of the count.

It is very important to determine the correct exposure time in making enlargements since this time very definitely affects the quality of your print. A simple way to help determine the correct exposure is to use test strips. This is done by cutting small strips from the larger sheets of printing paper of the same type to be used for the enlargement. Place these strips over the most important part of the subject on the easel. Insert the strips one at a time, exposing them at various intervals of time. Make your first test at whatever time you might guess to be near the correct exposure. Develop the strip to the full time recommended. If it is too dark or too light, make other tests over the same area, increasing or decreasing the exposure for a set amount of time. Be sure to keep in mind the amount of time required for the exposures. Run the fully developed test strips through the short stop and hypo. Turn on the room lights and check the results. (Make sure all unexposed or undeveloped printing paper is covered.) By comparing the strips, you can see the effects of the different exposures. You can easily see what the correct time should be. Now you can proceed to make a full size print. Be sure to develop it at the recommended time, just as the tests were developed. A few test strips allow you to get the correct time without using up an entire sheet of paper. After a little experience, you will be able to guess exposure more accurately, and you will be using fewer and fewer test strips.

Also available is a exposure test device that is placed over the printing paper and given a standard exposure of 60 seconds. Pie-shaped wedges are registered on the print to demonstrate the effect of different exposure times.

Printing papers are graded according to contrasts to provide the best possible prints from negatives of varying densities and contrasts. Most "average" negatives can be printed on "average" printing paper with acceptable results. The average paper is usually the #2 grade, but this will vary with papers made by different manufacturers. Some of them make paper that requires a #3 grade to print a negative that is printed satisfactorily on #2 grade paper made by other manufacturers. To obtain the best results from all negatives, it is desirable to keep a few different grades of paper on hand.

In recent years multi-contrast or "polycontrast" printing papers have become increasingly popular. These papers provide the control of various paper grades, without the need of several boxes of paper. The paper contrast is controlled by making the exposure through filters. These filters are available to fit any enlarger as well as contact printers.

The beginning photographer usually wants to print the full contents of his negatives on small size prints. Later, he ventures into bigger enlargements and he learns that he can crop out portions of the negative to improve the finished picture. Sometimes this calls for extreme enlargements; often larger than the normal capacity of the enlarger. Extra lenses are often the answer to bigger than normal blow-ups, or when small portions of the negative are enlarged. Also some enlargers can be turned to project on the wall or reversed to project the image onto the floor rather than the baseboard. Your capacity for enlarging is only limited by the size of the room.

The most common way of making large blow-ups is to turn the enlarger baseboard backwards on the worktable, while the head of the enlarger is turned on its post. This will project the image onto the floor. The baseboard will have to be weighted down with heavy boxes or other objects to counterbalance the weight of the enlarger head. Place your easel on the floor to hold the printing paper during the exposure. If the enlargement is very great, the distance from the enlarger to the paper might be too far to focus the enlarger easily. This usually will require the help of one other person. One person turns the focus knob while the other watches the projected image for sharpness.

You will find the exposure time will be increased with an increase in enlargement size. To shorten this time for ease of operation you can replace the normal 75-watt enlarger bulb with a larger bulb, such as the 150-watt or 250-watt bulb.

Always check your focus closely when making big enlargements requiring a long exposure. The long exposure may cause the negative to buckle in the negative carrier, naturally throwing it out of focus in spots. This will only be noticed in glassless carriers.

BLACK & WHITE ENLARGING PAPERS

PAPER	TYPE	SPEED	WEIGHT
AGFA-GEVAERT			
Brovira	Enlarging; neutral-black tone	Fast	SW, DW
Portriga Rapid	Enlarging; warm tone	Medium	DW
DUPONT			
Emprex	Enlarging; warm tone; single grade	Medium	DW
Mural	Enlarging	Fast	MW
Varigam	Enlarging; variable-contrast; cold tone	Medium	LW, SW, DW
Varilour	Enlarging; variable contrast; variable image tone (blue-black to warm black)	Fast	LW, SW, DW
Velour Black	Enlarging; cold tone	Fast	LW, SW, DW
GAF			
Allura	Enlarging; warm tone; single grade	Medium	DW
Cykora	Enlarging; warm-black tones	Medium	SW, DW
IIndiatone	Enlarging; warm-black tone; single grade	Slow	SW
Jet	Enlarging; cold tone	Fast	SW, DW
Panchromatic Type 3500	Enlarging; panchromatic; warm tone; single grade; requires dark amber No. 10 safelight filter or processing in complete darkness	Medium	DW
Panchromatic Type 3000	Enlarging; panchromatic; neutral tone; single grade	Fast	SW
Projection Proof	Enlarging; warm-black tone; single grade	Medium	SW
Vee Cee Rapid	Enlarging; variable contrast; cold tone	Fast	LW, SW, DW
ILFORD			
Ilfobrom	Enlarging; neutral tone	Fast	SW, DW
Ilfoprint	Enlarging; stabilization-type neutral tone	Fast	SW, DW
KODAK			
Ektalure	Enlarging; brown-black tone; single grade	Fast	SW, DW
Ektamatic SC	Enlarging; stabilization-type; variable contrast; warm black tone	Medium	SW
Kodabromide	Enlarging; neutral-black tone	Fast	LW, SW, DW
Medalist	Enlarging; warm-black tone	Medium	SW, DW
Mural	Designed for photo murals and large prints	Fast	SW
Panalure	Enlarging; panchromatic; warm tone; single grade; requires dark amber (No. 10) safelight filter or processing in total darkness	Fast	SW
Panalure Portrait	Enlarging; panchromatic; warm tone; single grade; requires dark amber (No. 10) safelight filter or processing in total darkness	Nearly medium	DW
Polycontrast	Enlarging; variable contrast; warm-black tone	Medium	LW, SW, DW
Polycontrast Rapid	Enlarging; variable contrast; warm-black tone	Moderately fast	SW, DW

PAPER	TYPE	SPEED	WEIGHT
Polycontrast Rapid RC	Enlarging; variable contrast; warm-black tone; water-resistant stock	Moderately fast	MW
Portrait Proof	Enlarging; single grade	Slow	SW
Portralure	Warm tone; variable contrast	Moderate	DW
Resisto Rapid	Enlarging; water-resistant stock	Fast	SW
Resisto Rapid Pan	Panchromatic enlarging; water-resistant stock	Fast	MW
LUMINOS			
Bromide Commercial F	Enlarging; black tone	Moderate	SW
Universal F	Enlarging; black-tone	Moderate	SW
RD Resin-coated	Enlarging; high-gloss white or velvet-matte	Moderate	SW
Bromide Double Weight	Enlarging; black tone, glossy, semi-matte, matte, crystal-grain	Fast	DW
Bromide Super Gloss F	Enlarging; extra whiteners; black tone	Fast	SW
Linen (cloth)	Enlarging; linen cloth; black tone; single grade	Medium	Cloth
Linon-T	Enlarging; warm tone; single grade; linen-type surface	Medium	DW
Mural	Enlarging; brown tone; single grade	Medium	MW
Pastel	Enlarging; red, blue, green, yellow, gold, silver stock; single grade	Moderately fast	SW
Portrait Charcoal-R	Enlarging; warm tone; single grade	Medium	DW
Portrait, DeLuxe Rapid	Enlarging; warm tone, white, cream-white, silk	Medium	DW
Portrait Proof	Enlarging; brown-black tone; single grade	Medium	MW
Portrait Tapestry-X	Enlarging; burlap-type surface; single grade	Medium	DW
SPIRATONE			
Colorbrome	Enlarging; yellow, orange, red, green, blue stock; single grade	Medium	SW
Goldbrome	Enlarging; gold stock; single grade	Medium	DW
Enlarging Paper	Enlarging; neutral black tone	Fast	SW, DW
Postcard	Enlarging; on postcard stock; single grade	Fast	DW
Psychobrome	Enlarging; fluorescent red, green, yellow stock; single grade	Medium	SW
Rapid	Enlarging; stabilization-type	Medium	SW, DW
Silverbrome	Enlarging; silver stock; single grade	Medium	DW
Special Surfaces	Enlarging; Crystal and Silk Sheen (neutral black tone), Oxford Black and Tapestry (warm tone)	Fast	DW
UNICOLOR			
Elizabeth F	Enlarging; blue-black	Medium	DW
Gigi E	Enlarging; blue-black	Medium	DW
Nicol N	Enlarging; blue-black	Medium	MW
Robin G	Enlarging; warm-black	Medium	MW
Sara Y	Enlarging; blue-black	Medium	MW
Victoria F	Enlarging; blue-black	Medium	SW

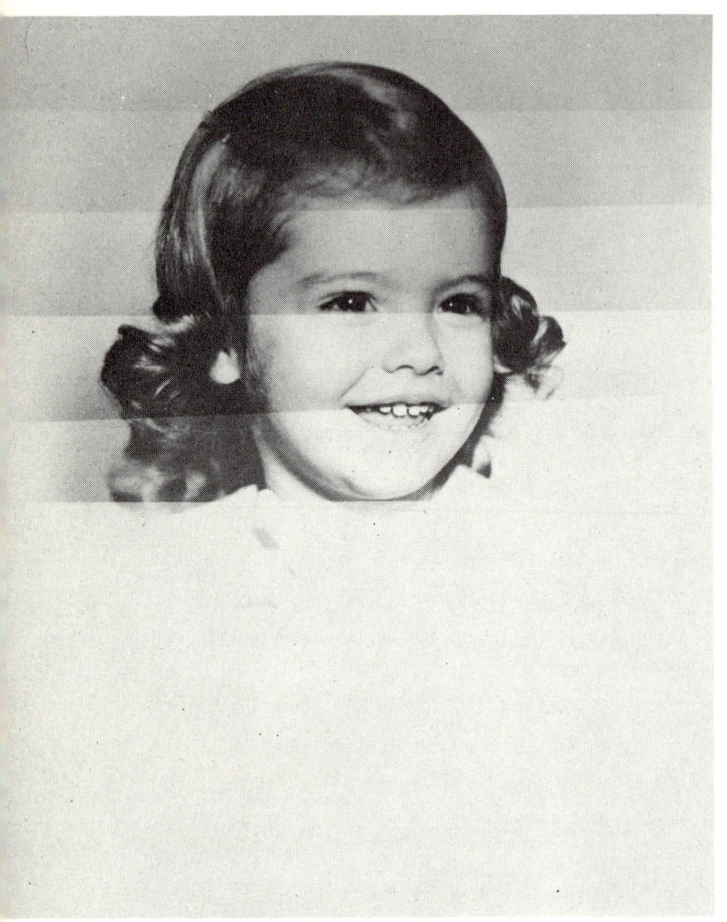 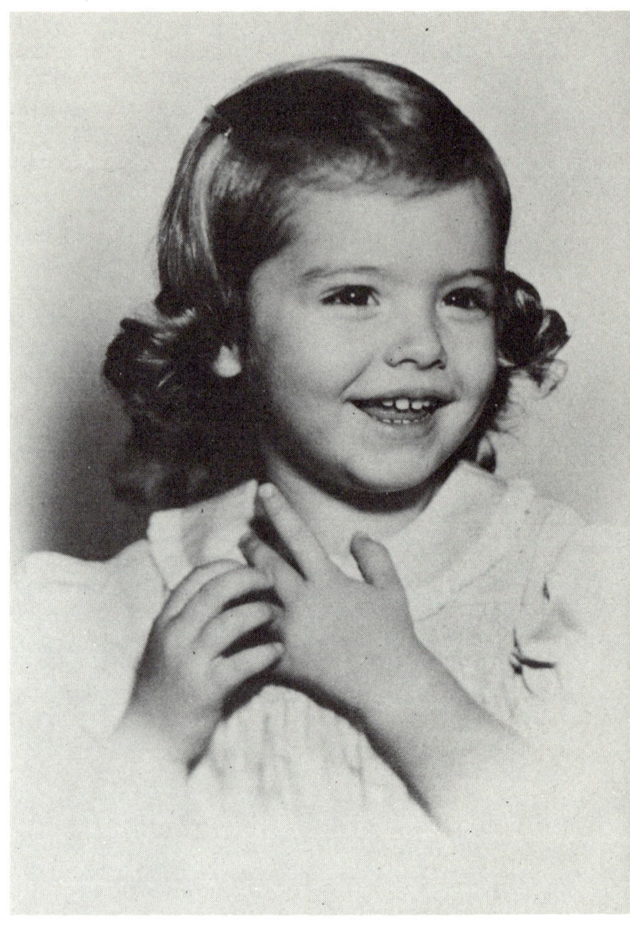

TEST PRINTS

Correct print exposure should be determined beforehand for every enlargement you make. One method demonstrated above is to move a piece of cardboard across your print in 5 or 10 second increments. Develop the print normally and examine it for the area that represents the subject as you wish it represented. In the example above, the photographer settled on the area containing the eyes in his test print. Another method of determining correct print exposure is to use the Kodak Projection Print Scale as demonstrated at the top of the opposite page. An exposure of 1 minute is given and the section showing the correct tonality is chosen for the final print. The wedges imprinted on the scale are of different densities to produce exposures in the various sections equivalent to the exposure times indicated. One method eliminates the need for the test print entirely. A print meter is placed on the enlarger baseboard as shown at the bottom of the opposite page and a reading is taken with the negative in position.

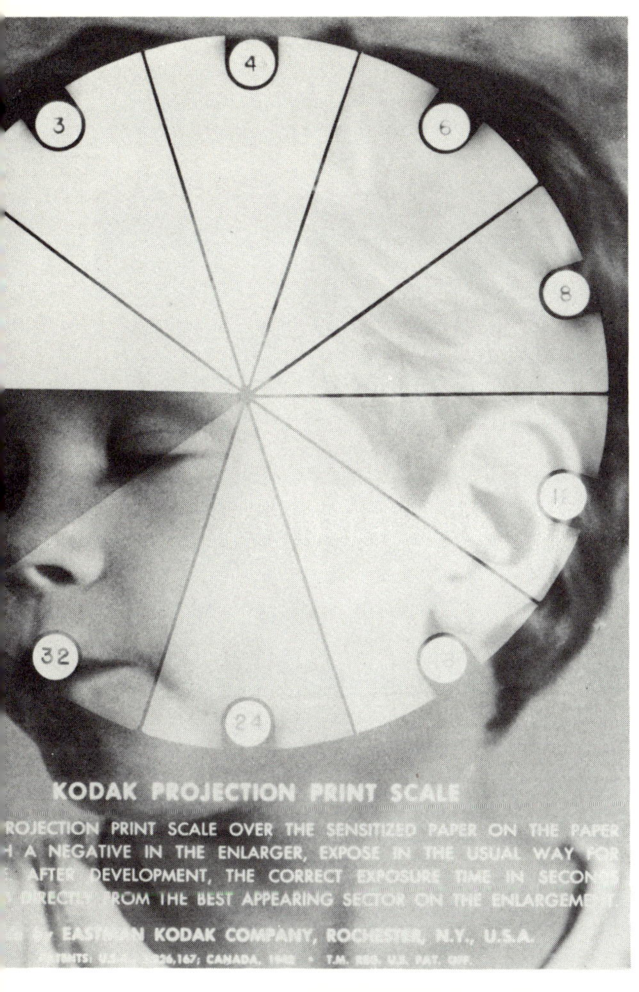
KODAK PROJECTION PRINT SCALE
ROJECTION PRINT SCALE OVER THE SENSITIZED PAPER ON THE PAPER
A NEGATIVE IN THE ENLARGER, EXPOSE IN THE USUAL WAY FOR
AFTER DEVELOPMENT, THE CORRECT EXPOSURE TIME IN SECONDS
DIRECTLY FROM THE BEST APPEARING SECTOR ON THE ENLARGEMENT.
EASTMAN KODAK COMPANY, ROCHESTER, N.Y., U.S.A.
PATENTS: U.S.A. 2,326,167; CANADA, 1942 • T.M. REG. U.S. PAT. OFF.

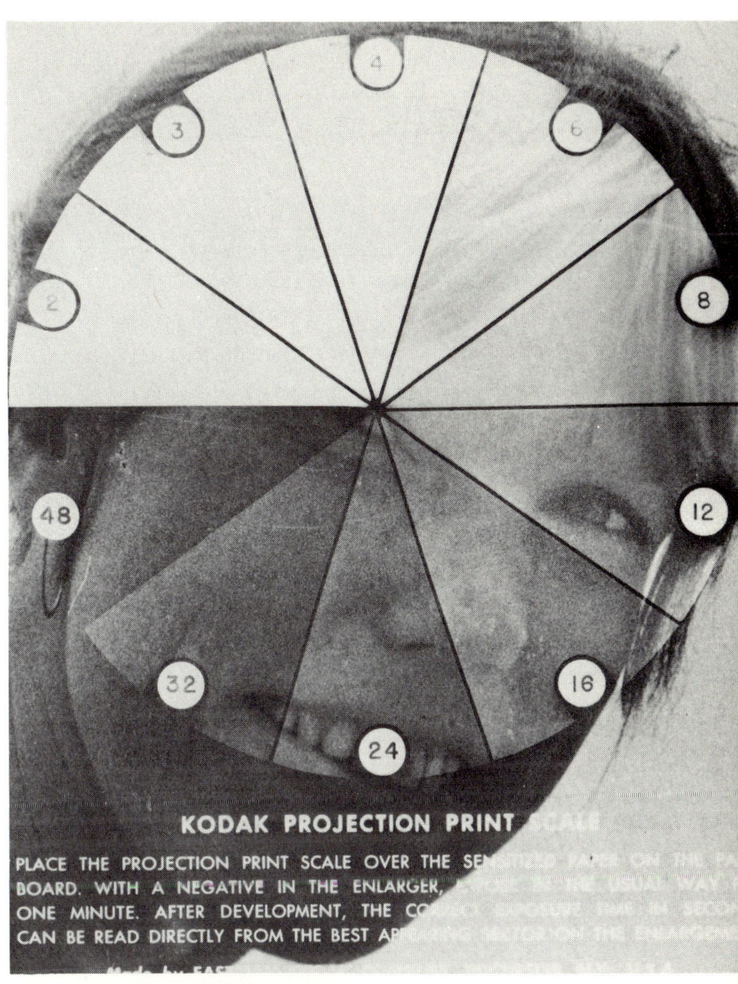
KODAK PROJECTION PRINT SCALE
PLACE THE PROJECTION PRINT SCALE OVER THE SENSITIZED PAPER ON THE PAPER
BOARD. WITH A NEGATIVE IN THE ENLARGER, EXPOSE IN THE USUAL WAY FOR
ONE MINUTE. AFTER DEVELOPMENT, THE CORRECT EXPOSURE TIME IN SECONDS
CAN BE READ DIRECTLY FROM THE BEST APPEARING SECTOR ON THE ENLARGEMENT.
Made by EAST

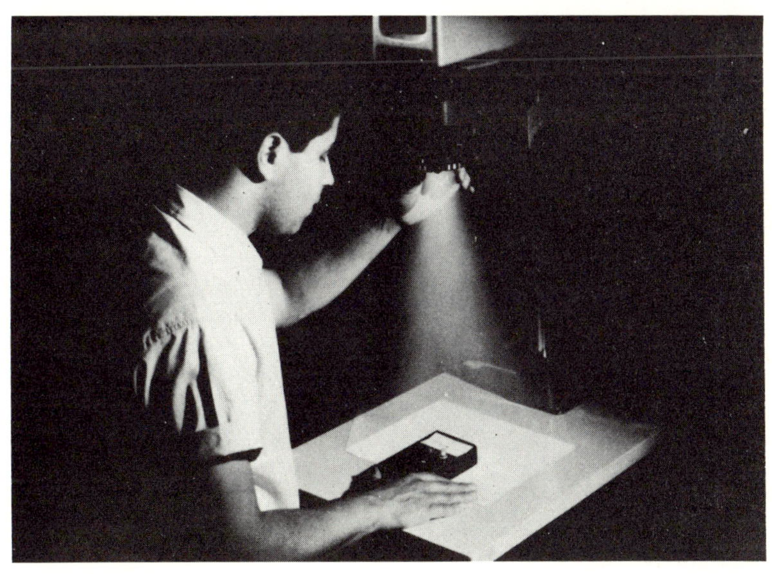

EXPOSURE CONTROL

The effect of gradually increasing exposure time is shown in these prints. The exposure increased from the first print at top left, across the top row, and through the bottom row to the last print at bottom right. The fourth, fifth, and sixth prints could all be considered normal while the seventh print might be the choice if the photographer wished for a

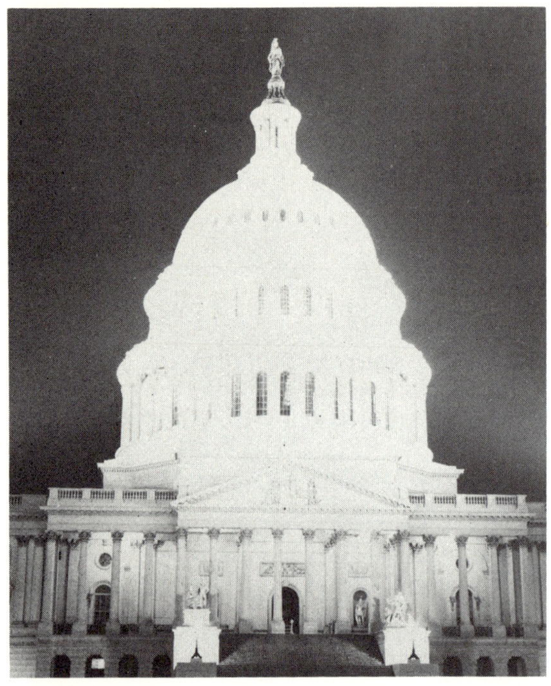
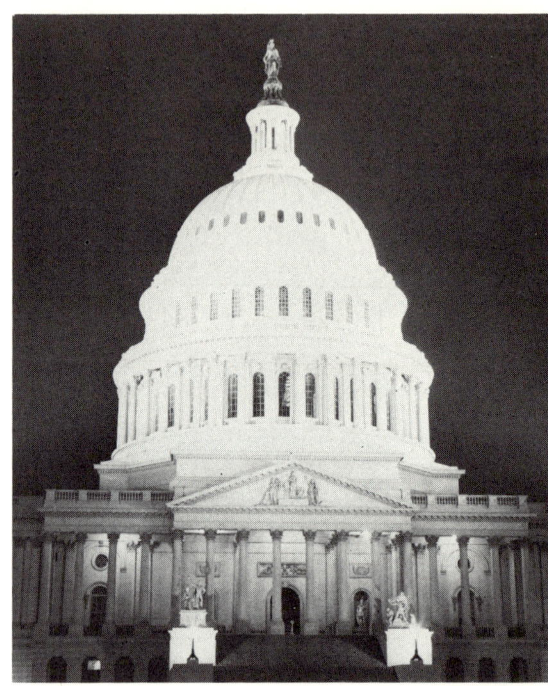
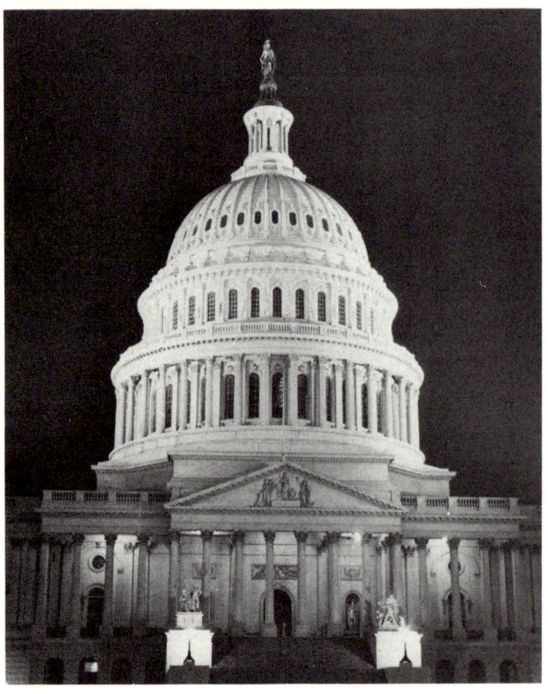
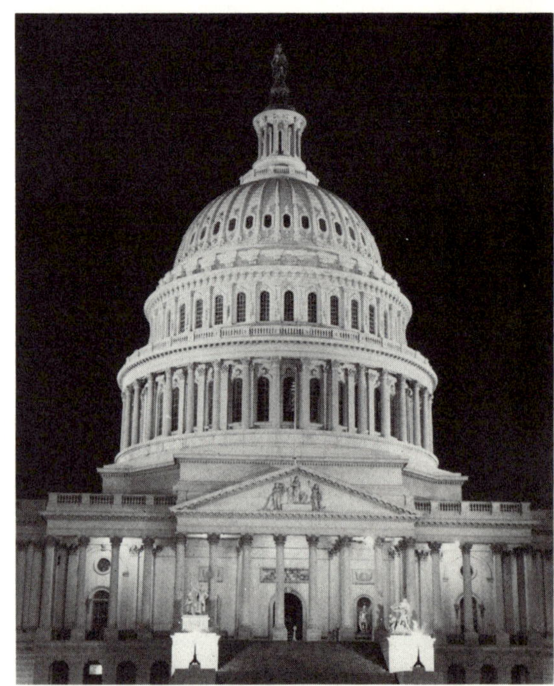

dramatic night quality. Once you have established the "correct" exposure for a print, mark the lens opening and exposure time on the back of the print so you can repeat the effect without further trial and error.

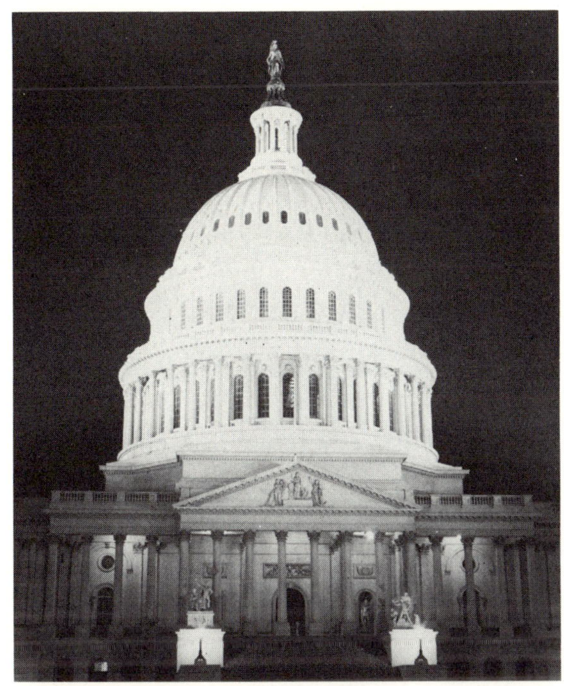

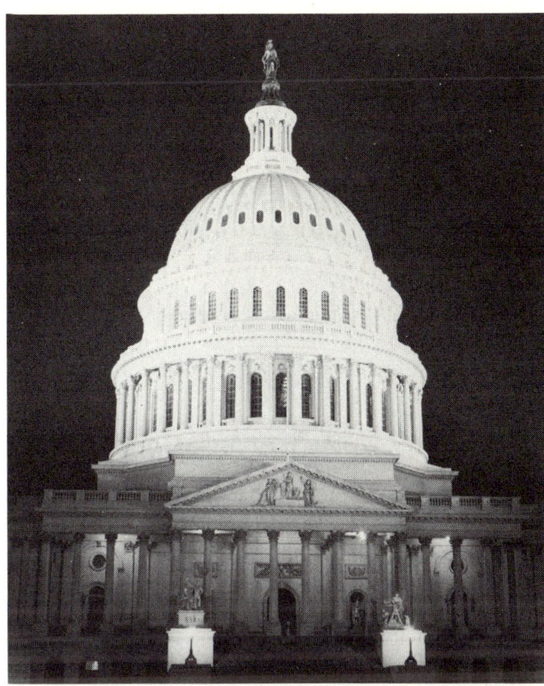

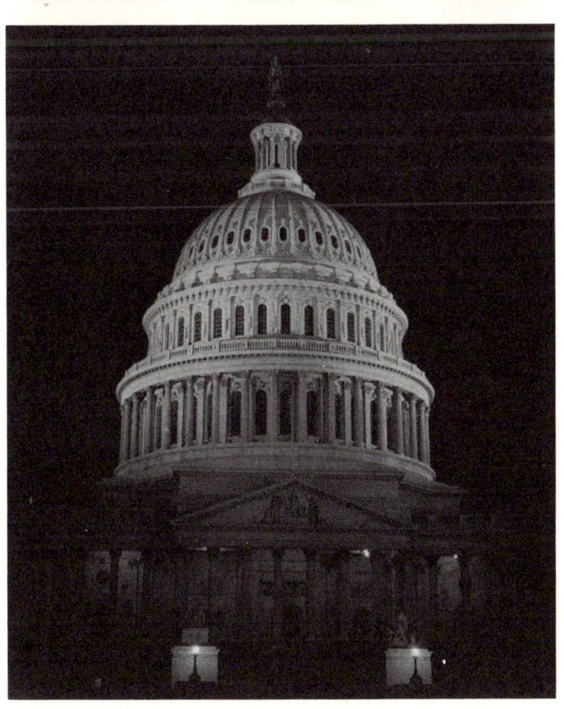

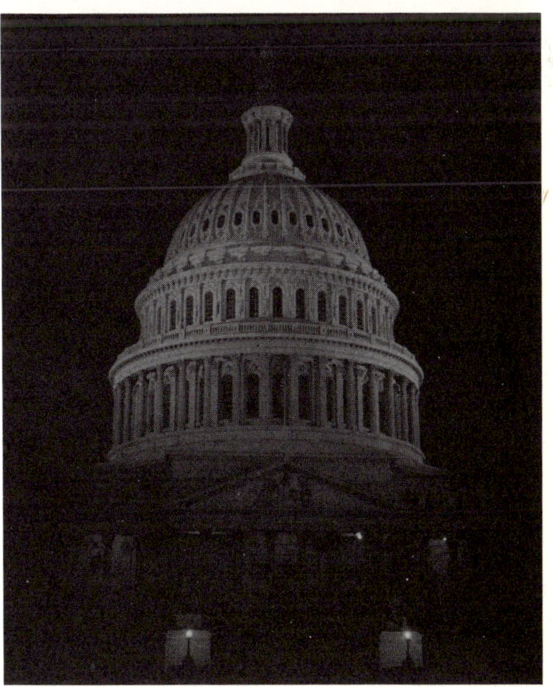

POLYCONTRAST PRINTING

A single box of paper was made to produce these prints of increasing contrast. The sequence runs across the top row then across the bottom from left to right.

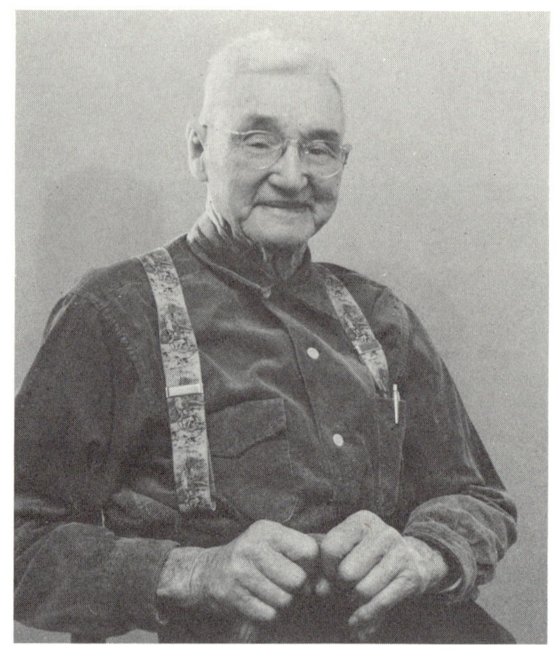

#1 polycontrast filter

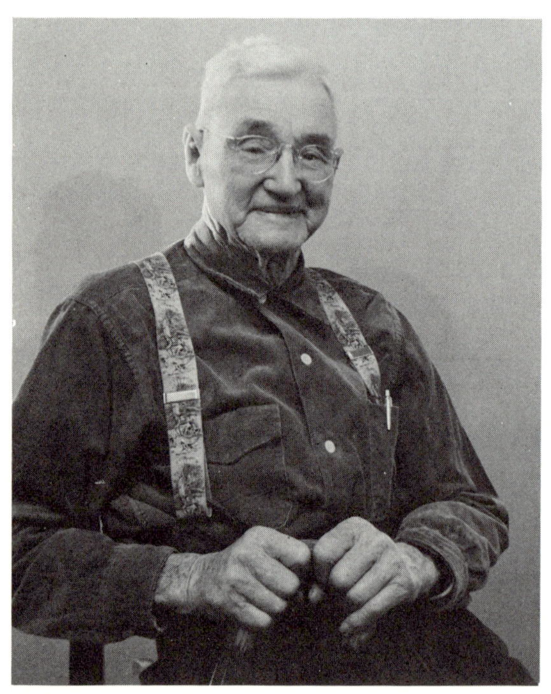

#2½ polycontrast filter

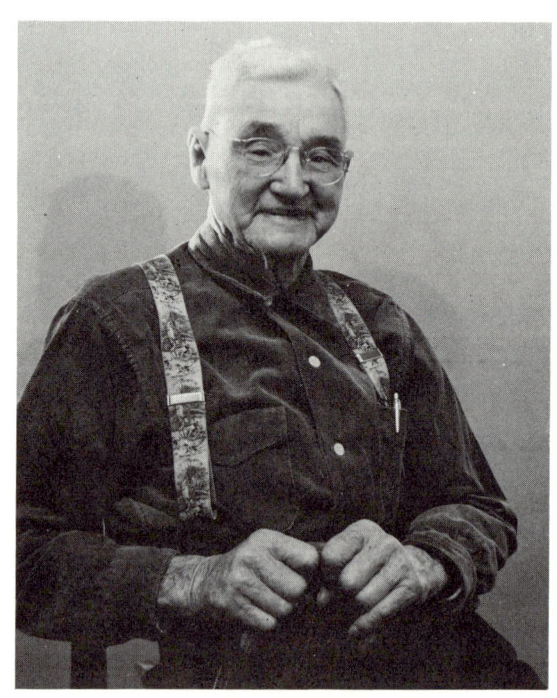

#3 polycontrast filter

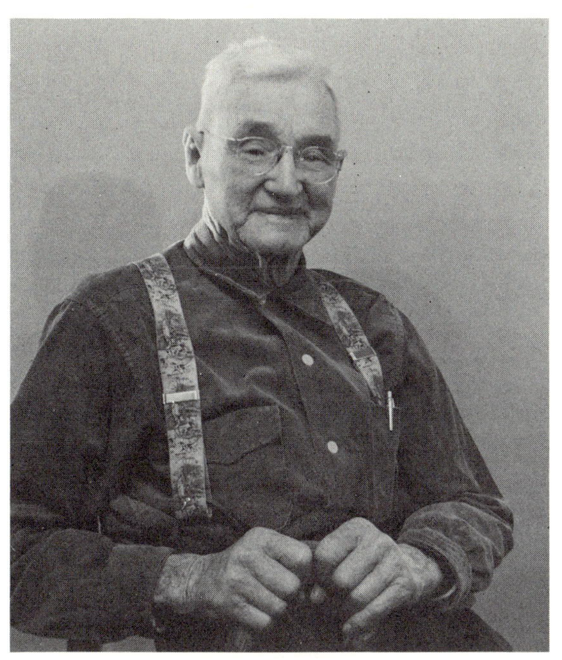

#1¹/₂ polycontrast filter

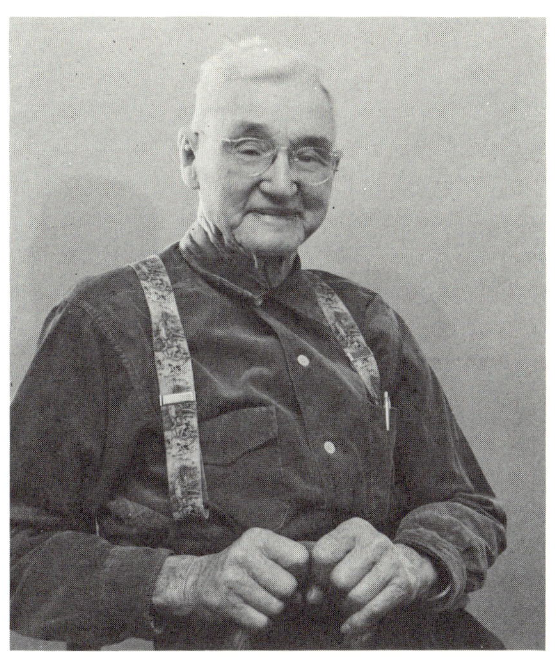

#2 polycontrast filter

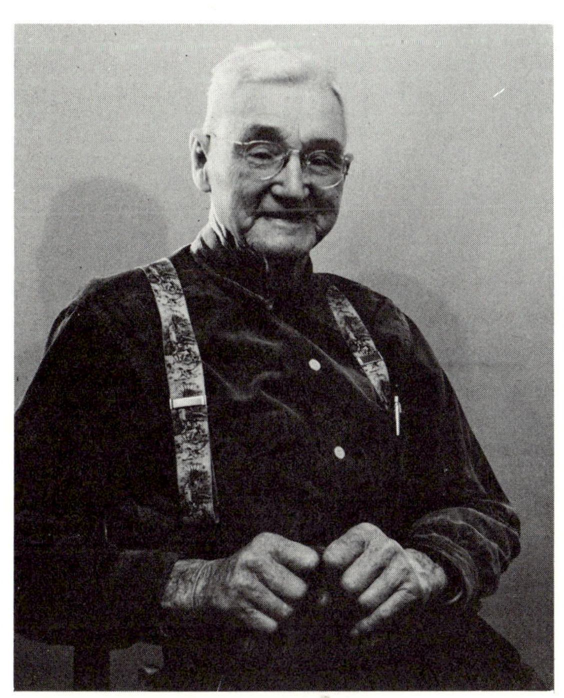

#3¹/₂ polycontrast filter

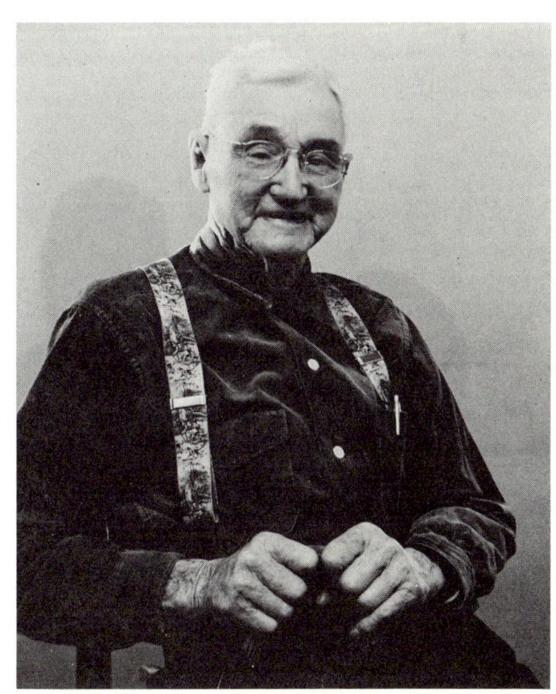

#4 polycontrast filter

The beginning photographer may have good results in making contact prints, with no troubles from dust spots and scratches; but as soon as he starts to make enlargements he finds these added hazards. Tiny particles of dust and minute scratches on the negatives are enlarged to the same degree as the rest of the negative. The enlarger can really make mountains out of molehills.

Some of these spots can be removed on the finished print by spotting or retouching; but this is tiring, boring, time-consuming work. Any measures you can take to avoid the need for it are well worth the effort. The time and trouble spent in maintaining cleanliness in developing and printing will be much shorter than the time needed to fix up prints done in a careless way.

Static electricity is one of the major causes of dust. It makes films draw airborne and surface particles like a magnet. This can be remedied to some extent by using an anti-static rinse and wetting agent. You simply use it instead of your regular wetting agent in the final rinse, just before drying your film. It can also be used to coat the negative carriers of your enlarger to help repel dust prior to and during the process of making the enlargement. Metal negative carriers sometimes will build up a static charge and attract dust particles. These static charges can be caused to bleed off into the air by coating the holders thinly with anti-static solution, which is invisible and has no other effect. It is best to coat the inside surfaces of the holder, so the treatment will not be subject to wear from handling. It can be applied very easily with a cotton dauber.

It is in the printing process that the negative is subjected to the greatest amount of handling and quite a few print defects can be caused at this point. Thorough cleaning of the enlarger is necessary before starting a darkroom session. The lens should be brushed clean with a soft camel's hair brush. It should be checked again as you continue your work, especially in extended printing sessions. If dust appears again, the lens should be wiped clean again. There is one type of brush available with a built-in blower. It has a rubber bulb for a handle. Just squeeze the handle to blow away dust particles that are hard to reach with the brush (such as around the edge of the lens).

Don't forget to clean the diffuser lens of your enlarger. The different elements can collect dust and make mysterious smudges and lines on your enlargements.

Regardless of how much brushing you may do to clean your negative you are very likely to have dust spots on the negative when it is placed in the enlarger. Brushing generates static electricity, attracting more dust. You can stop most of this trouble by grounding the enlarger. Run a wire to a nearby water pipe and connect the wire to the enlarger by an alligator clip, or loosen a screw somewhere and attach the wire. This ground will lessen the number of dust specks on the enlargements, since the static charge will dissipate when you insert the metal negative carrier into the grounded enlarger.

If particles of dust have dried onto the film, after settling on wet film hanging to dry, they can usually be removed with a liquid cleaner such as carbon tetrachloride. Dampen some cotton with the cleaner and lightly rub the negative.

Sometimes it is difficult to see dust particles and especially lint on negatives in the low level of illumination of the darkroom. If the negative is held obliquely in the path of light projected by the enlarger, dust particles are clearly visible. You can also keep a flashlight handy to edge-light your negative for the same effect. Be sure all printing paper is covered to protect it from fogging from the white light of the enlarger or the flashlight.

All your efforts in trying to keep down dust will be in vain if dust-filled air is being drawn into the room by your ventilating system. For best results the room should be sealed as tightly as possible. Air intakes should be covered with filters of the type used in air conditioners and furnace ventilating systems. This should give a relatively dust-free atmosphere.

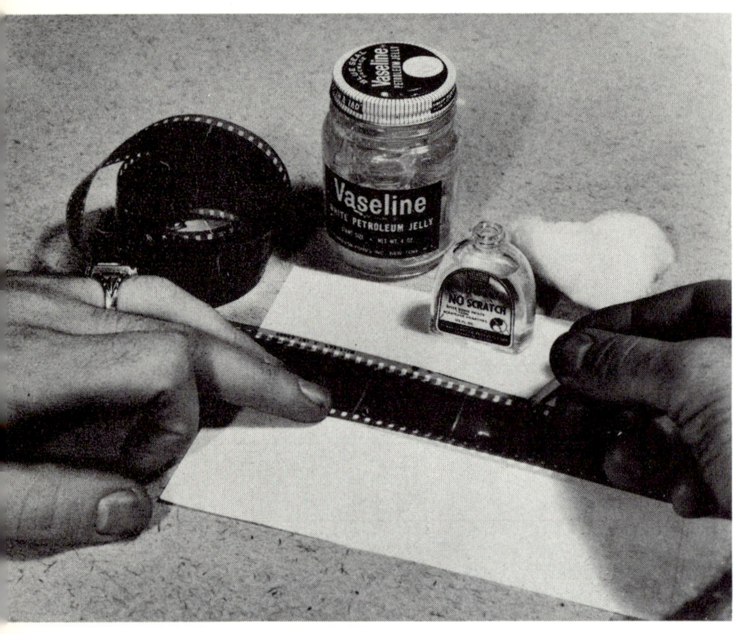

Scratches in the negative can be repaired by using
Vaseline or commercially available scratch remover. After
the scratches are repaired, wipe the negatives gently with
a wad of cotton to remove any excess oil.
A poorly cared for negative was used to make the print at
the top of the opposite page. An excessive amount of
spotting would be necessary to make this print present-
able. The lower print was made from the same negative
after it was cleaned and its scratches were repaired.

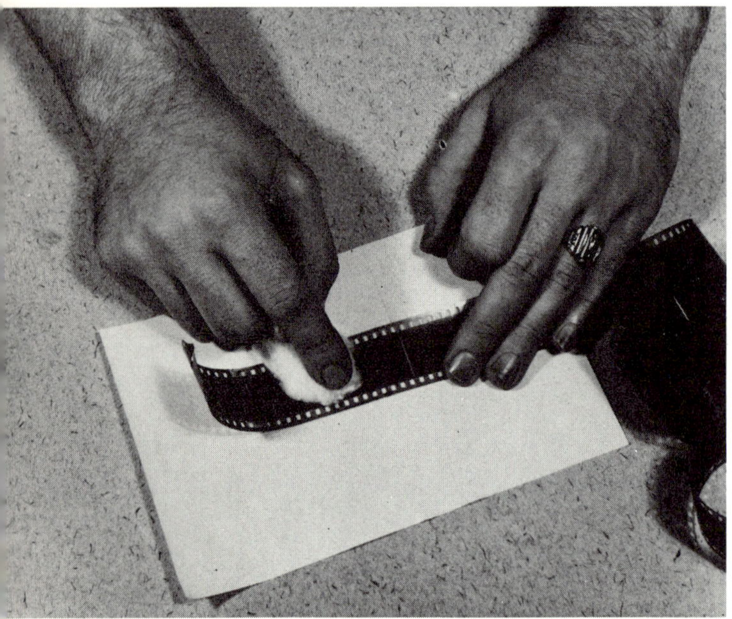

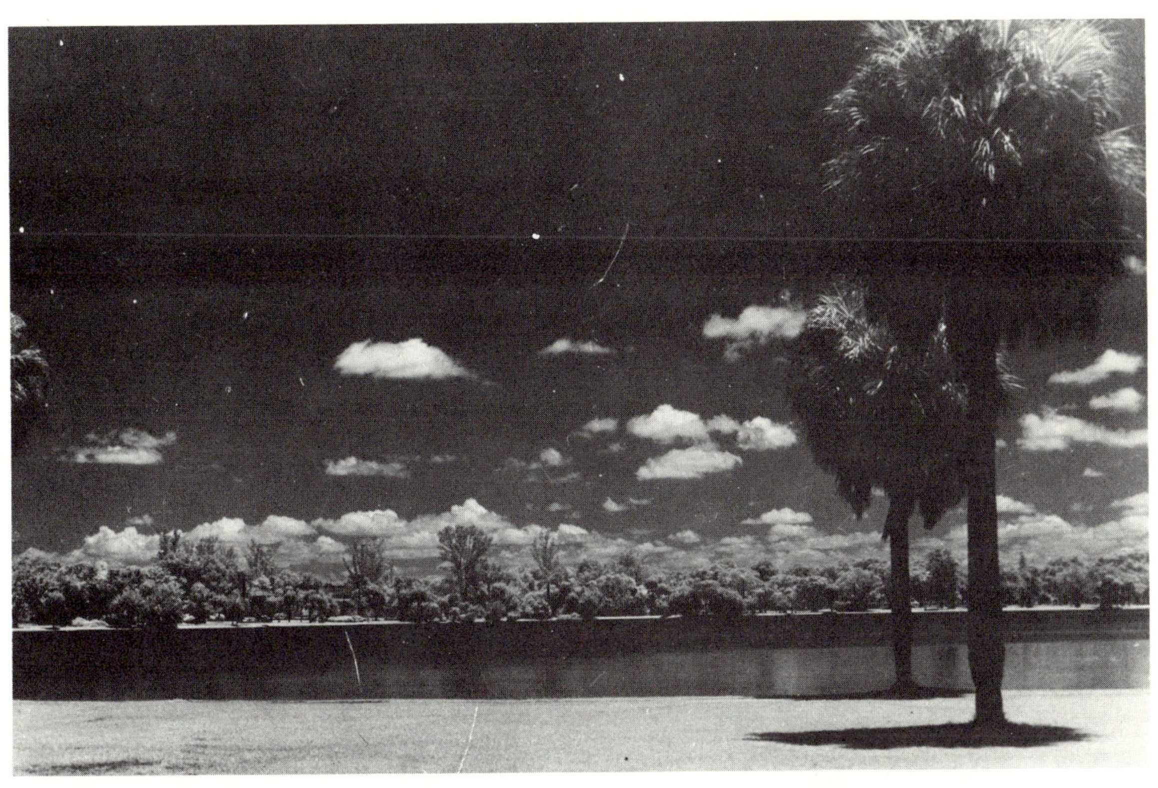

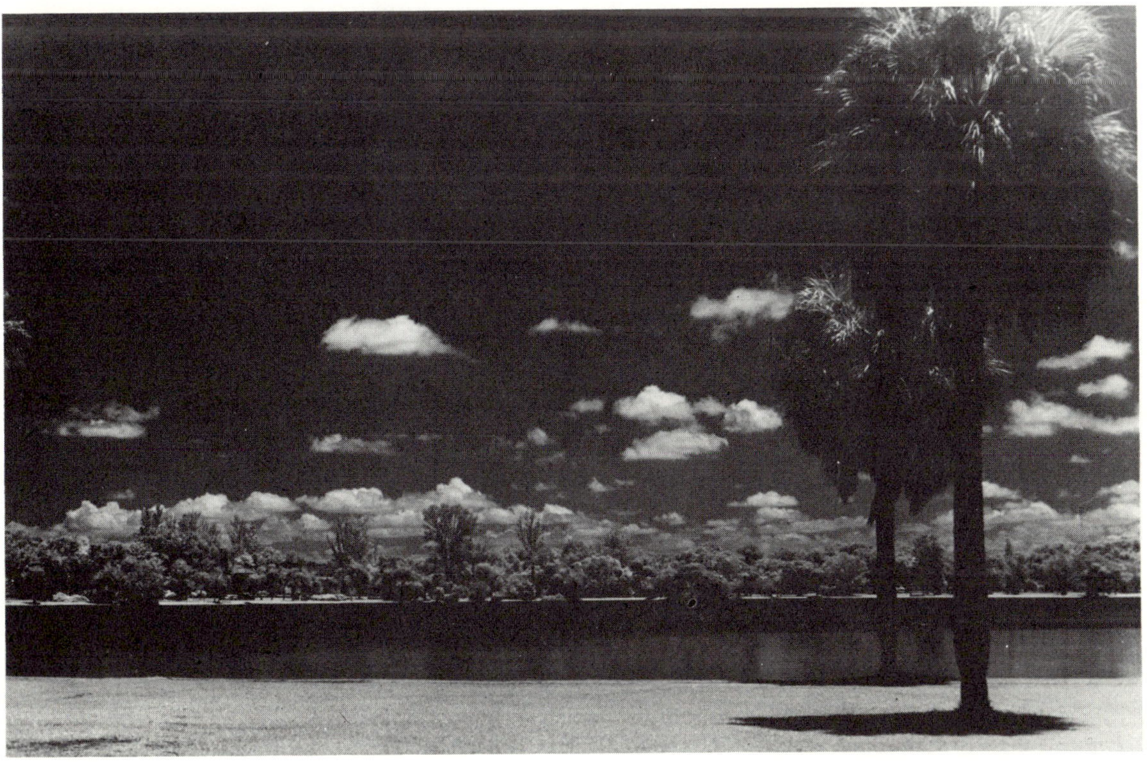

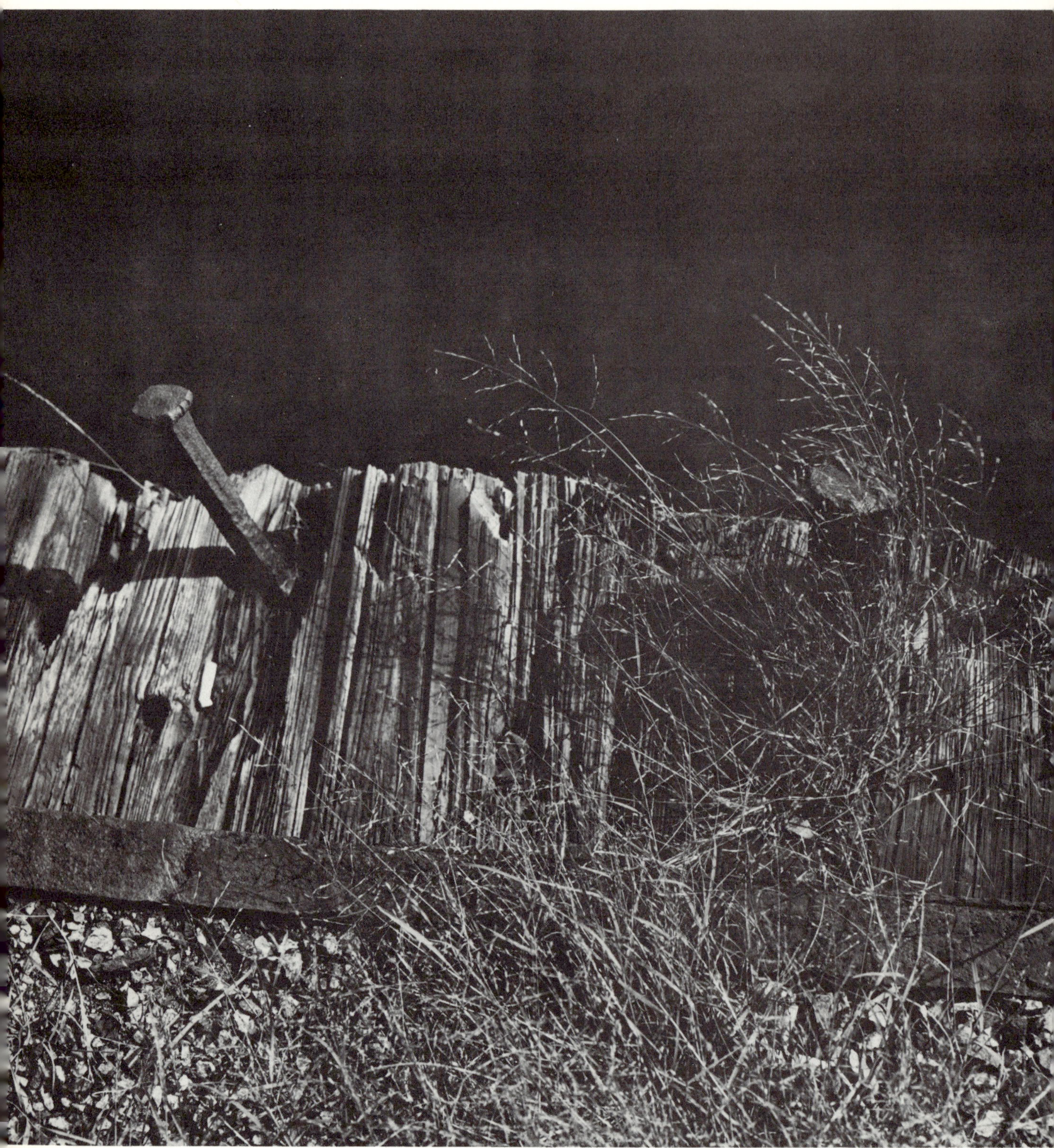

DEVELOPING THE PRINT

A correctly exposed print should reach to proper tonality at the full developing time recommended in the developer instructions. Print development is no place to make up for exposure deficiencies. A good, fully developed print will feature tones from black to white like those in the print reproduced on the opposite page.

DEVELOPING THE PRINT

"How can I make prints with the sparkle and quality of those pictures that I see made by the professionals? I have good negatives, good equipment; I use fresh chemicals and paper, and yet my prints are usually gray and dull when finished. They just don't have that 'oomph' that I know they should have to do justice to the negative." These are common questions and complaints of many amateur photographers.

Print quality is a common problem with the majority of amateurs, yet there are others with seemingly no better equipment who equal or even outstrip the pros in print quality. A very simple way for the darkroom worker to improve his darkroom output is to observe a strict darkroom routine. Most amateurs just don't go to the trouble to read and follow directions to the letter. By using the basic information given by manufacturers anyone can master the fundamentals of good darkroom technique. Such things as exposure time, temperature of solutions (both while mixing and while in use), dilution of chemicals, agitation, prevention of contamination, etc., are all important. These are overlooked by a large percentage of amateurs trying to make good pictures, and they wonder why their prints don't turn out as they should. Usually they blame the paper, chemicals or anything else they can think of. Many give up in exasperation, yet the answer to their problem is usually right at their fingertips.

Developing of prints is actually the most fascinating part of photography. It continues to draw your interest regardless of how much you have done, since it is the culmination of all previous efforts combined to produce the final print. This step is really not so complicated. Standardization is very important. If the beginner starts out learning the rules and following them, he will have better results, and it will be more fun as he sees good pictures come out of his efforts.

One of the first rules is to be absolutely clean in your work. First of all, wear old clothes or an apron to protect your clothes from any chemical splashes.

Contamination is a big problem that often goes unrecognized. Many workers fail to realize the effect that stop bath or hypo has on print quality when accidentally mixed into the developer. Many student workers put their hands into the developer after having placed them in the stop bath or hypo (fixer) tray. From that point on, the developer will only produce prints with a gray mottled appearance. Even the smallest trace of hypo in the developer will tend to cut the tonal quality of a print. The best idea is to have individual sets of tongs for each tray. The developer-tray tongs are used for moving the print in the developer then picking it up and dropping it into the stop bath. Stop-bath tongs transfer the print to the hypo and hypo-tray tongs are reserved for manipulation in and removal from the hypo. Like hands, tongs must not be contaminated. A second suggestion is to have a sink handy for washing the hands or at least a tray containing clean water to be used as a finger rinse. Rinse the hands completely before going back into the developer. Above all, do not dry your hands on a towel when they are covered with chemicals. This causes contamination every time you use the towel after that.

Dilution and the temperature of developer is something else that should always be constant. (Here again follow the manufacturer's instructions, which will vary with different developers and papers.) In many cases, the difference may be only slight, but usually is enough to knock the pep out of a print.

The basic steps of developing a print and carrying it through the stop bath and fixer can be learned by anyone. It is up to each individual to see that he learns these steps correctly in the very beginning.

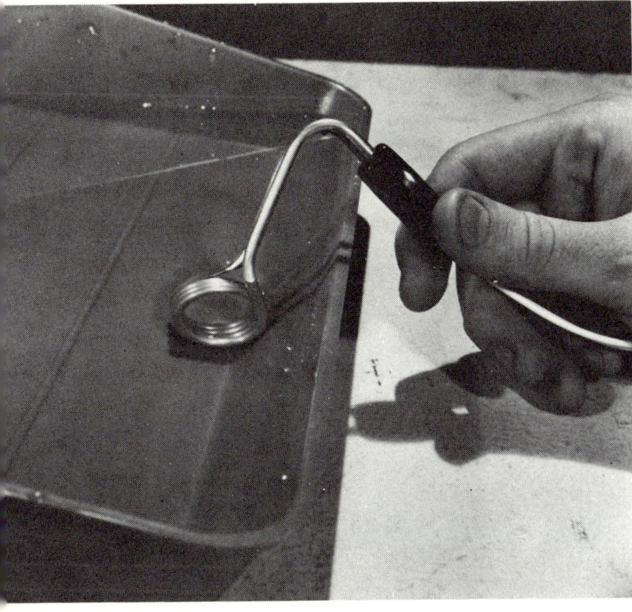

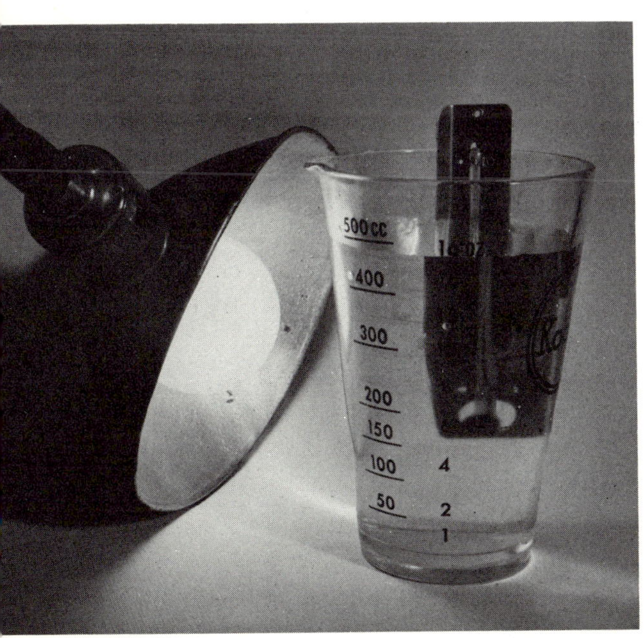

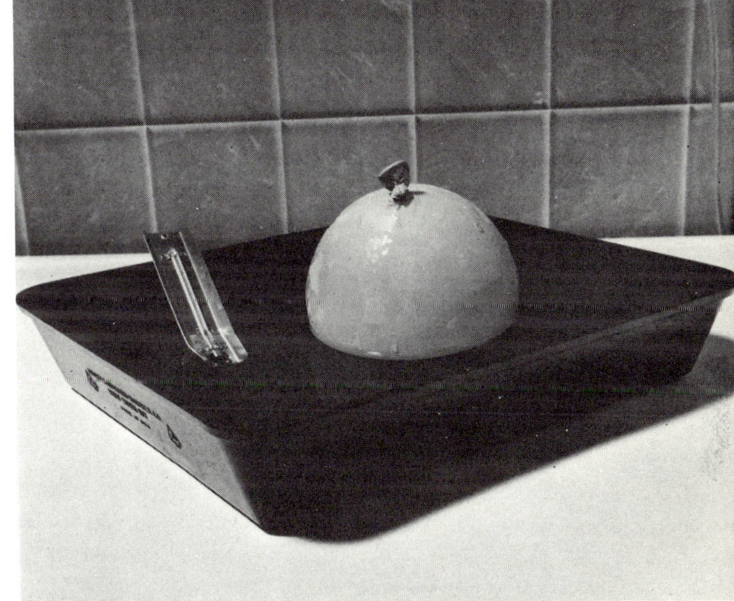

Developer should be used at the manufacturer's recommended temperature. Three simple techniques for adjusting developer temperature are shown here. At left, a heating coil is immersed in the developer. At the lower left, a glass beaker filled with developer is placed in front of a warming lamp. Below, a balloon filled with cold water then frozen in the refrigerator freezer compartment is used to cool developer.

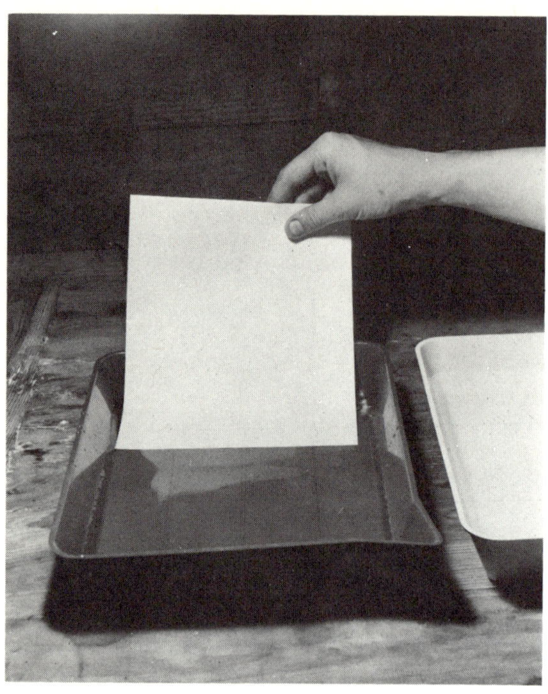

It is important to insert the print into the developer as quickly as possible and then to make sure that it is entirely immersed.

Tongs should be used to transfer the print from one tray to the next. Permit as much chemical as possible to drain from the print before transferring it.

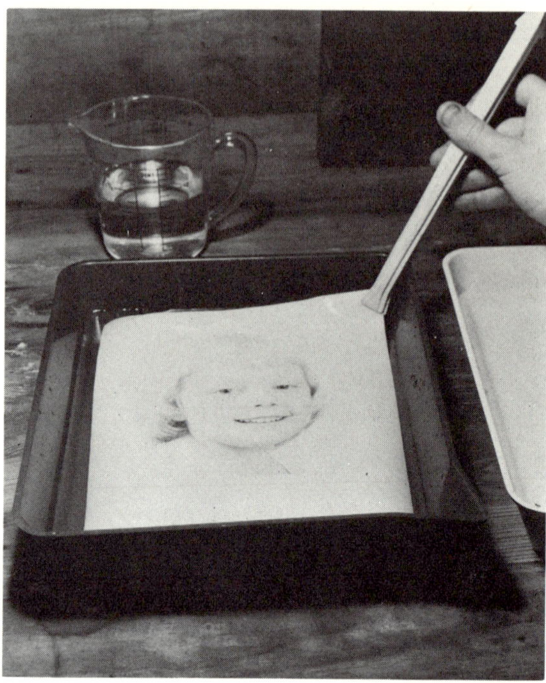

After about 30 seconds, a normally exposed print will start to appear.

The second developing step, the stop bath, causes no visible reaction in the print. It does however abruptly stop developer action. The print should remain in the stop bath for 6 to 8 seconds.

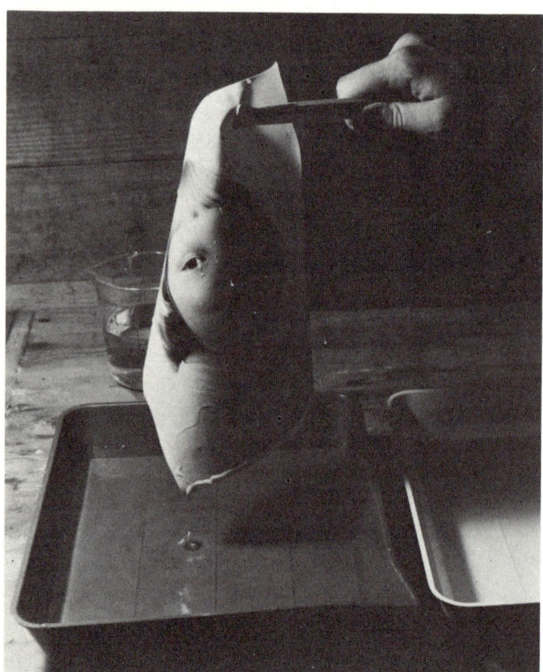

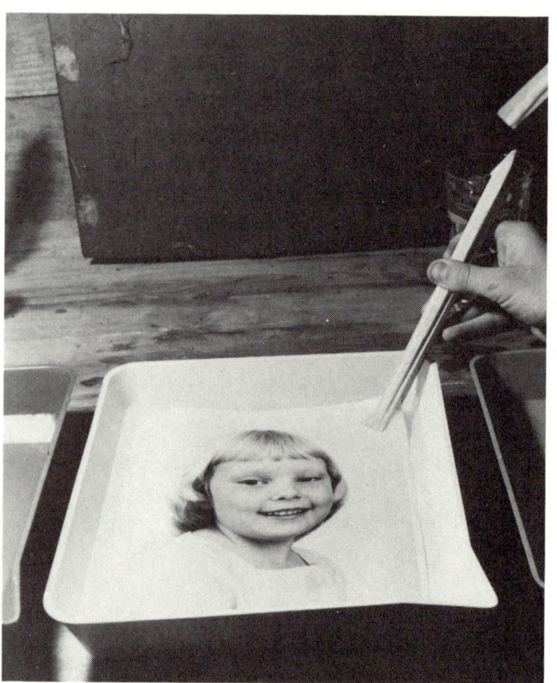

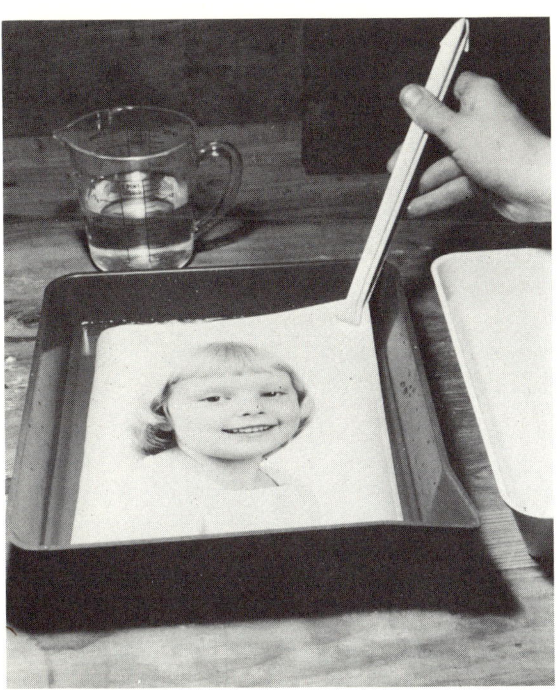

After about one minute the print is much more visible but not fully developed.

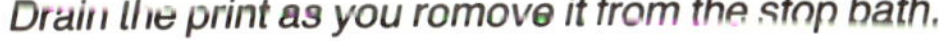

Drain the print as you remove it from the stop bath.

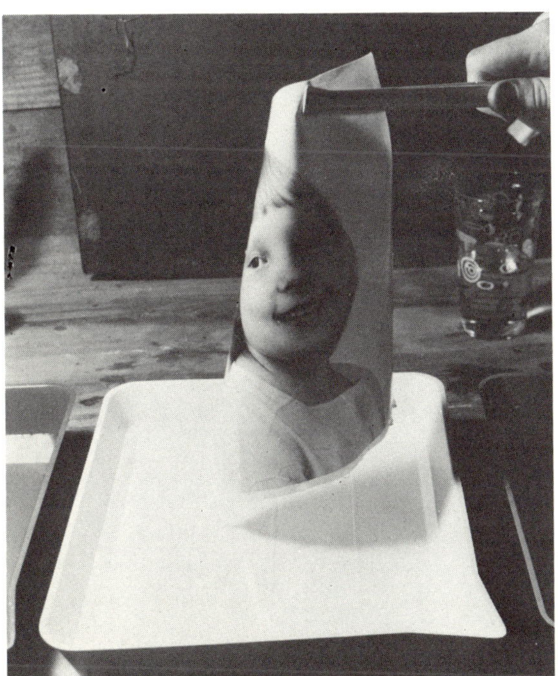

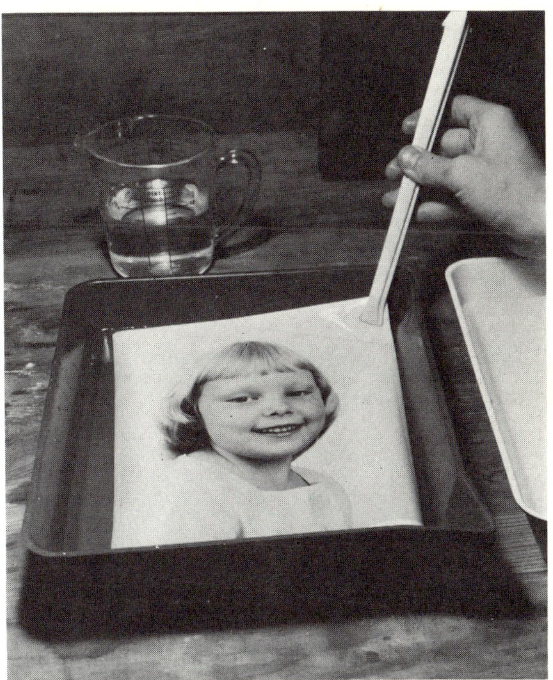

The print reaches its full richness only after full development.

Place the print in the fixer for the length of time recommended by the fixer manufacturer. Agitate the tray from time to time to assure even fixing. If the print tends to stay on the surface, turn it over and make sure it is completely submerged.

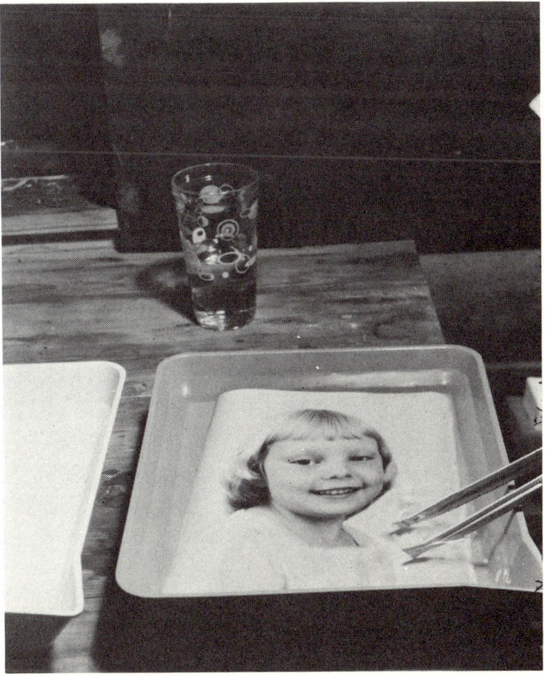

POPULAR PAPER DEVELOPERS

Acufine Printofine   supplied as powder

DuPont 53-D All Purpose
          Developer*   powder
          55-D Standard Paper
          Developer   powder

Edwal Platinum   liquid
       Super III   liquid
       TST   liquid

Ethol LPD   powder

GAF Ardol   powder
      Miradol WT   powder
      Vivadol*   powder

Ilford Bromophen   powder

Kodak Dektol   powder
        Ektonal   powder
        Selectol   powder
        Versatol   liquid

can also be used for film processing

Some photographers never go beyond the stage of making "straight prints," just ordinary pictures showing little or no imagination. But, with a little time and effort, the average darkroom worker can soon learn to pep up his pictures by little additions that lift pictures from the ho-hum variety to a beautiful end result that draws attention.

Dodging and local printing are two of the easiest and most common controls exercised on the enlargement. "Dodging" means holding back light areas of the negative that otherwise would print extremely dark. Dodging is carried out by placing an object of the necessary size between the lens and the enlarger easel to keep this area from receiving as long an exposure as the rest of the picture. A piece of wire with a paper or piece of cotton on the end will serve the purpose for small areas. By using your hand or a cardboard you can dodge large areas.

Local printing, or "burning in" as it is commonly called, means just the opposite of dodging. An area of the negative that needs more exposure is given more light than the rest of the print by exposing this particular area through a hole in a card, after the entire print has received the normal time.

Vignetting is accomplished in much the same way as burning in a particular area, except that the area including the subject is all that is exposed through the cardboard or vignetter. The area outside this center receives no exposure at all, and is allowed to go completely white. The picture gradually fades out at the edges into the white area.

In doing dodging or local printing, be sure to keep your dodger or cardboard mask moving slightly. If the wire dodger is allowed to stay in one spot for very long, the wire itself is liable to make a visible line on the print. Cardboard masks will also make a distinct separation line on the print if held still, although only a small amount of motion is necessary to diffuse the edges so they don't show.

Often the beginner does not get the full benefit of a good negative because he does not print dark enough to bring out the subject to best advantage. By mixing common sense with a little judgment and experience, you can more than likely make your pictures better by printing them darker. The trouble comes when deciding how dark to make the print. There is no rule-of-thumb, since the darkness of each print must be decided separately. Many times you will find it is possible to bring out qualities of texture and form to improve the picture, even though the tones may be deeper than they actually are in real life. Dig out some of your negatives and try printing them lighter or darker—you may be surprised at how many good pictures will result from negatives you considered not too good.

"Double printing" is a simple darkroom trick. It's fine to find a scenic setting capped by a "photographer's sky"—fluffy, white clouds that stand out prominently against a glorious blue background. Unfortunately, such a treat occurs all too seldom, and when it does, you can consider yourself lucky. More often, when you're in the mood to shoot landscapes, you run into a series of cloudless days that result in pictures with the dead look of a blank sky.

This is where you can do some rainy day work in the darkroom to improve those landscapes. You can print in beautiful skies at will if you have appropriate cloud negatives of various types. These can be added to those "baldheaded" scenics by a little manipulation in printing. You may find some good cloud negatives by looking through some of your old landscape shots that were never too successful because they lacked one thing or another in the foreground. Your best bet is to build a file of negatives by shooting pictures whenever you see a fine cloud formation of the type you normally would want in your photographs. Make pictures of clouds under various conditions—backlighted, sidelighted, and front-lighted clouds. You'll need all of them in your file, in order to be able to choose a negative showing clouds lighted in character with your scene.

After selecting a suitable cloud formation that seems to fit in with the particular scene you are printing, you are ready to begin. Place your scenic negative in the enlarger and proceed to make a test strip. After developing the test strip and determining the correct exposure time, you can expose the scenic part of the picture (foreground). Place this piece of paper in a print box until you are ready to expose the cloud portion onto the print. Be sure to mark the back of the piece of paper so that you will know which direction is up when you get ready to expose it again.

Next place a piece of cardboard over the projected image of the scene, and draw a line along the horizon of the picture. Cut the cardboard along this line. The bottom part of this cardboard is to be used as a dodger to hold back the foreground while the clouds are projected and printed onto the same piece of paper that you have already exposed.

Now take the scenic negative out of the enlarger and replace it with the cloud negative. Compose the cloud negative into the top portion of the easel, making sure it falls into the area not covered by the foreground picture. Make the test strip of the clouds, developing the strip identically with the test for the foreground, since the final print will include the two exposures on the same piece of paper.

After determining an exposure that produces a good sky background in the correct developing time, you can expose the clouds onto the upper half of the half-exposed piece of paper. While doing this, use your cardboard dodger to prevent light from reaching the part of the print where you already have exposed the foreground.

There will be times when you can make the double exposure to insert clouds without the dodging manipulations. These are easy to do on scenes with dark skylines and dark subject material, such as a silhouette, but if you have foreground subject matter with odd shapes, they will be hard to shield during printing.

With a little care and experience you can use many controls of printing to change the whole feeling of a picture. Each picture requires personal attention, and only experience can teach you the correct methods for the best results. With these basic ideas in mind, you can spend a few rainy days in the darkroom and surprise yourself with the results.

"Diffusion" is a printing control usually reserved for portraits. It serves a very definite purpose—to diffuse the features that the camera sees so distinctly but which will not look so good if printed sharp and clear. The camera sees every line and blemish on a person's face in a closeup portrait. These blemishes are not so noticeable in real life, since we look at a person's face selectively, seeing only one area at a time, briefly. In a printed picture, we have a chance to see the whole face at once and all of the undesirable features seem to stand out if they are not toned down to some extent. In studio photography with large cameras, this is taken care of with retouching on the negative, but retouching is very limited on the average small negative. That's where diffusing lends a hand. By placing a wrinkled cellophane, an old stocking, or a wire screen diffuser between the enlarger lens and the printing paper for a portion of the exposure, the projected image is diffused slightly for that portion of the exposure time. This time will vary with the amount of diffusion necessary and can be determined by making trial exposures. Usually the diffusion-exposure time will be about $1/3$ of the overall exposure time. Your own tastes and needs will dictate the amount of diffusion you wish to use, and experience will tell you how much will be needed with your particular type of negatives.

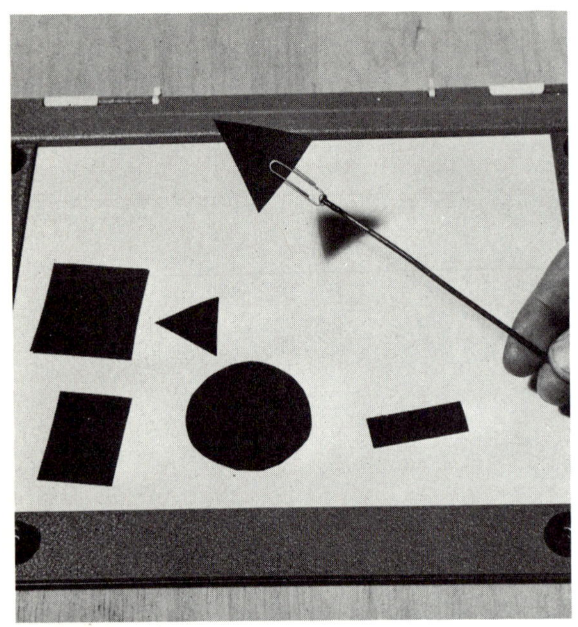

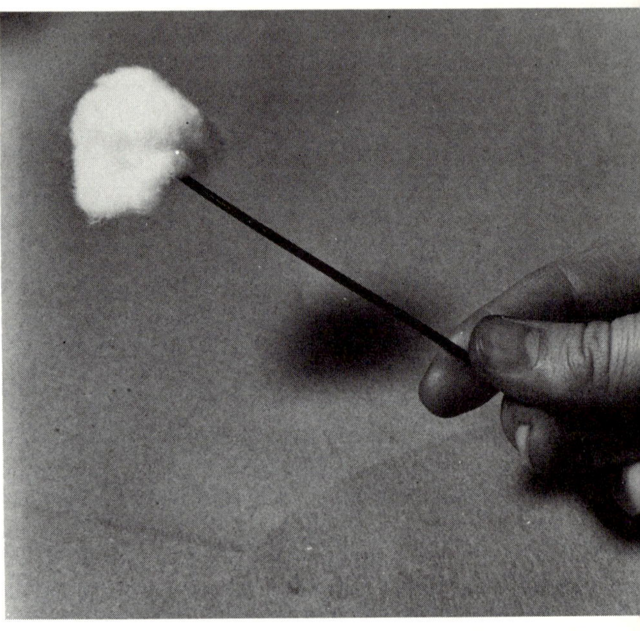

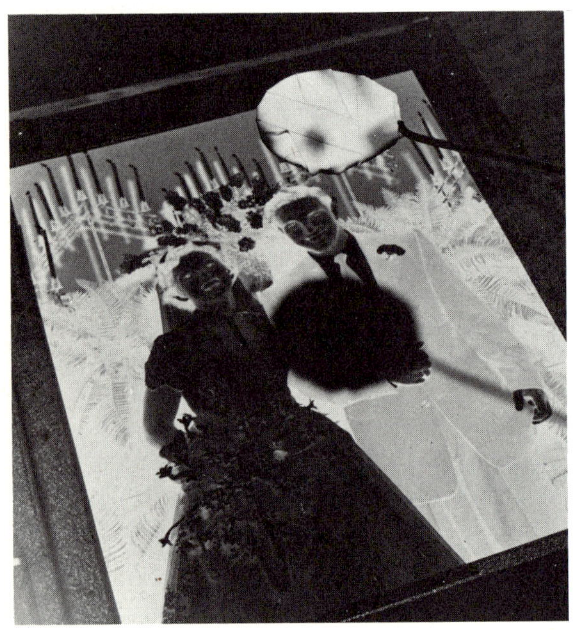

A paper clip attached to a short length of wire hanger can form the foundation of a versatile dodger. Different shapes of cardboard can be attached (as shown above at left). A wad of cotton mounted on a wire (as shown above) can also serve as a dodging tool. The effect of the dodger is shown in the print at left. Exposure is being held back from a very thin area of the negative. The print on the opposite page was dodged in the area of the cat's face to maintain the detail of the eyes.

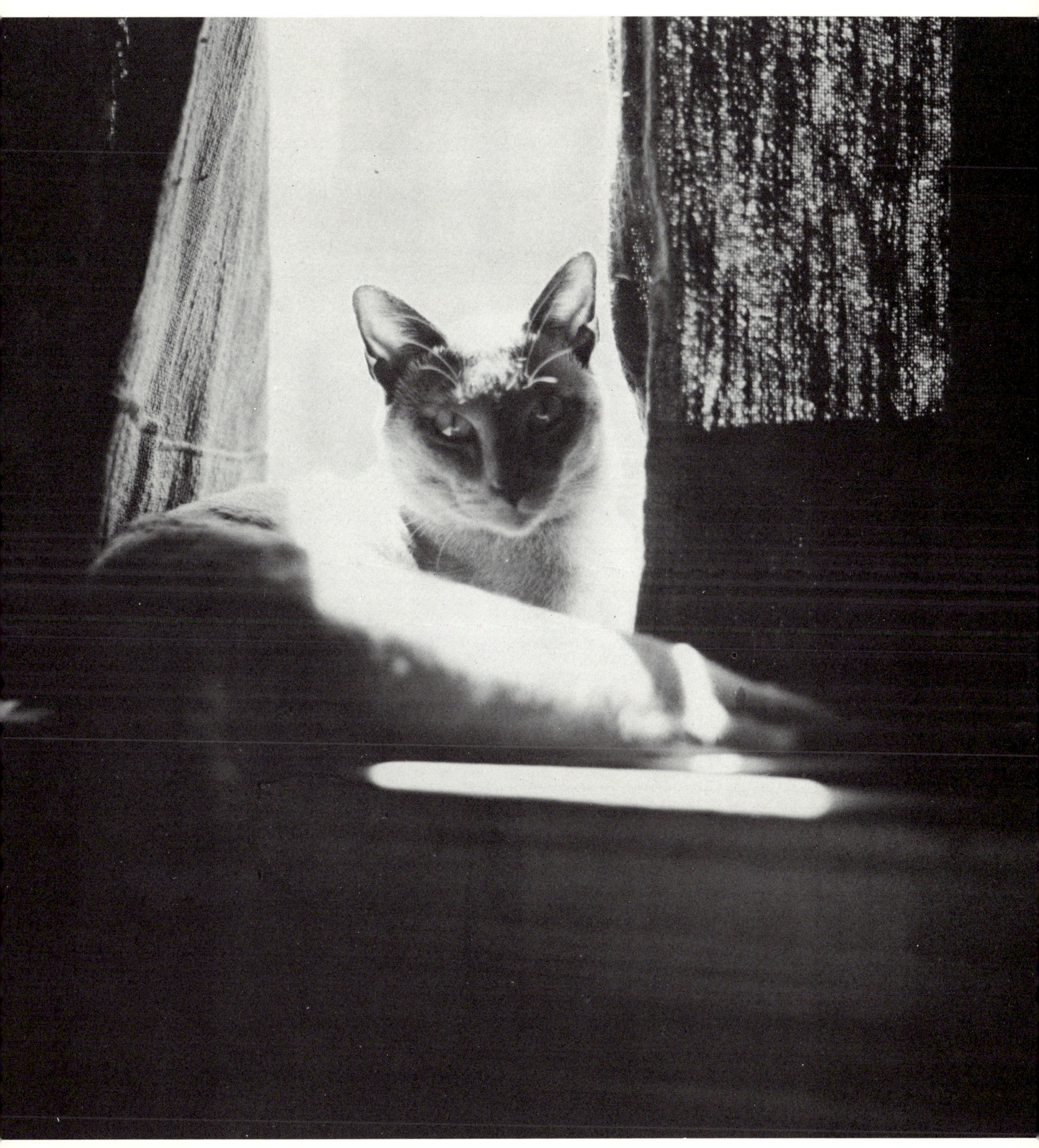

VIGNETTING

Vignetting allows the photographer to reproduce only a section of the negative with the perimeters going gradually light or dark.

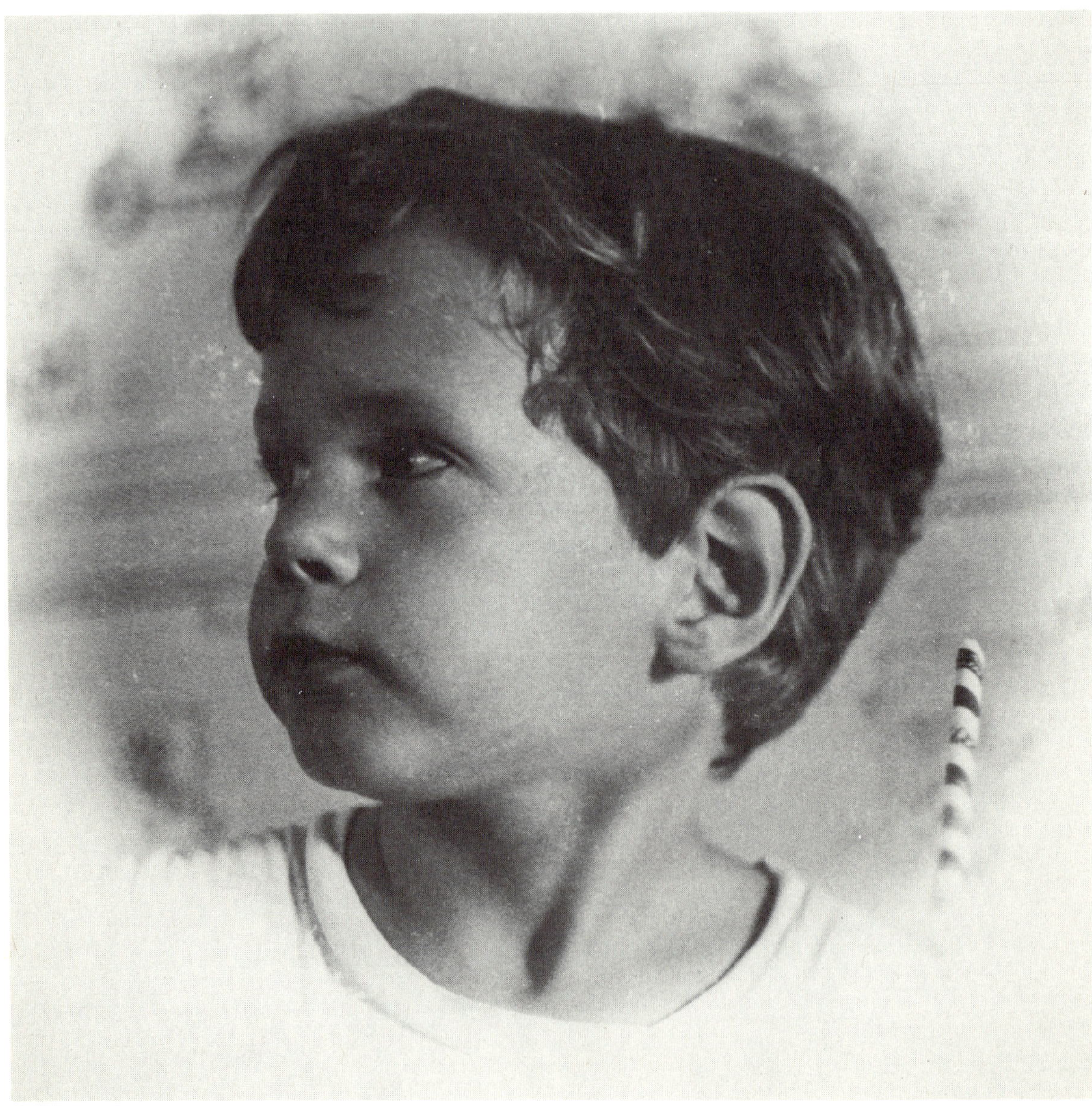

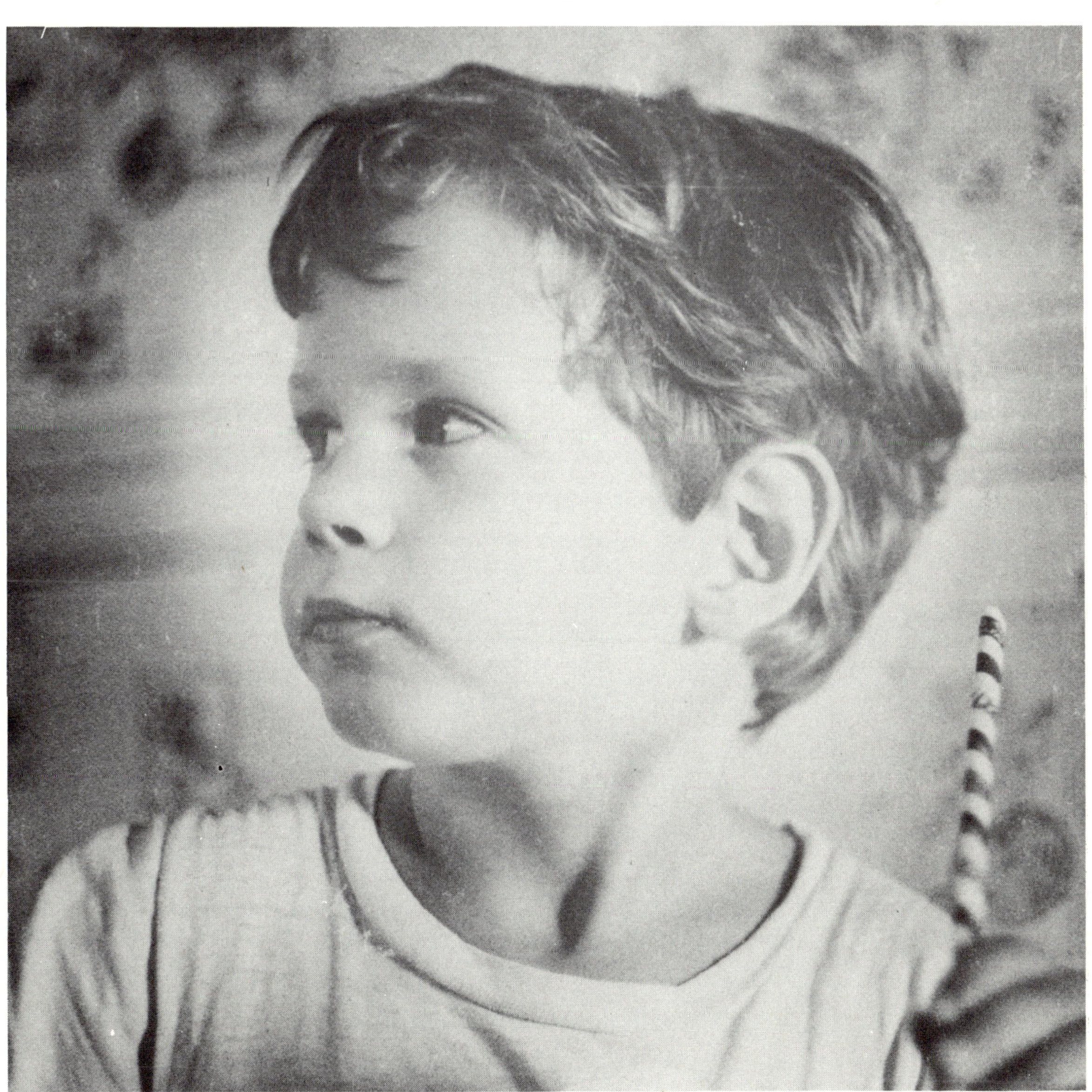

DOUBLE PRINTING

Double printing can be used both correctively and creatively. In the print at right, the empty sky is distracting. Additional exposure for the sky area (below left) did little to correct the situation. For the final print (below right) a normal printing exposure was made for the park and trees. Then, the exposed area was covered to prevent further exposure, a negative showing clouds was put in the enlarger, and the clouds were printed in.
The prints on the opposite page demonstrate the dramatic potential of double printing.

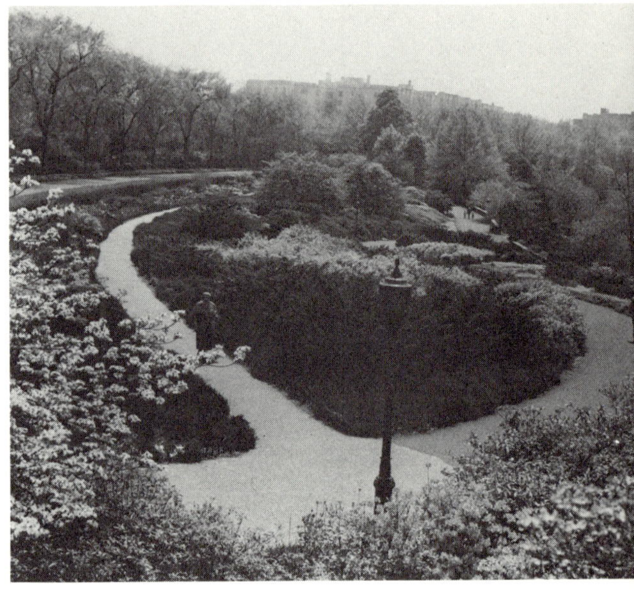

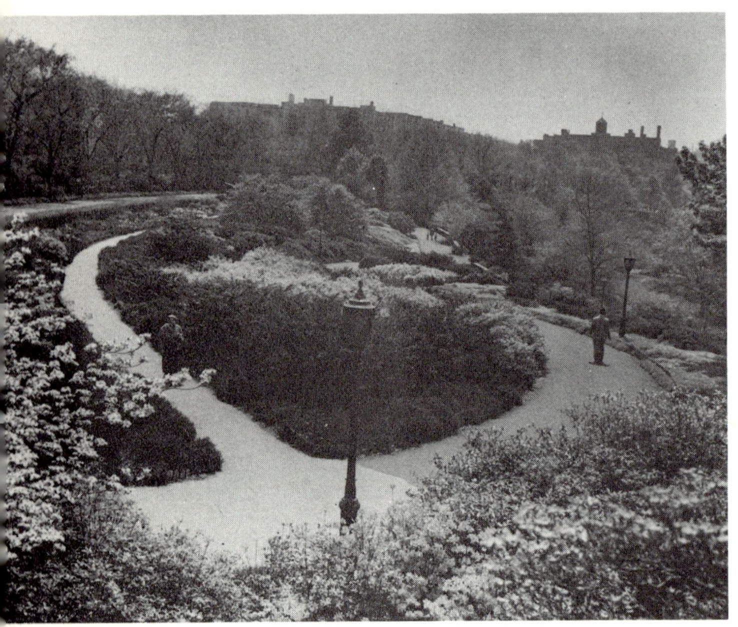

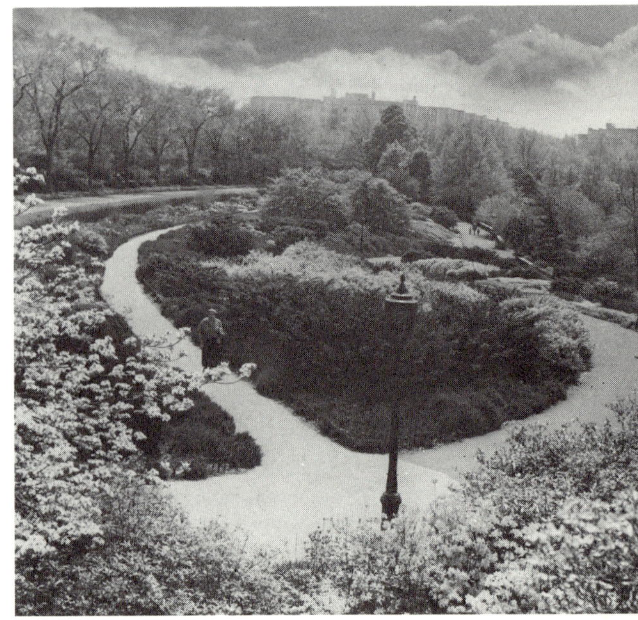

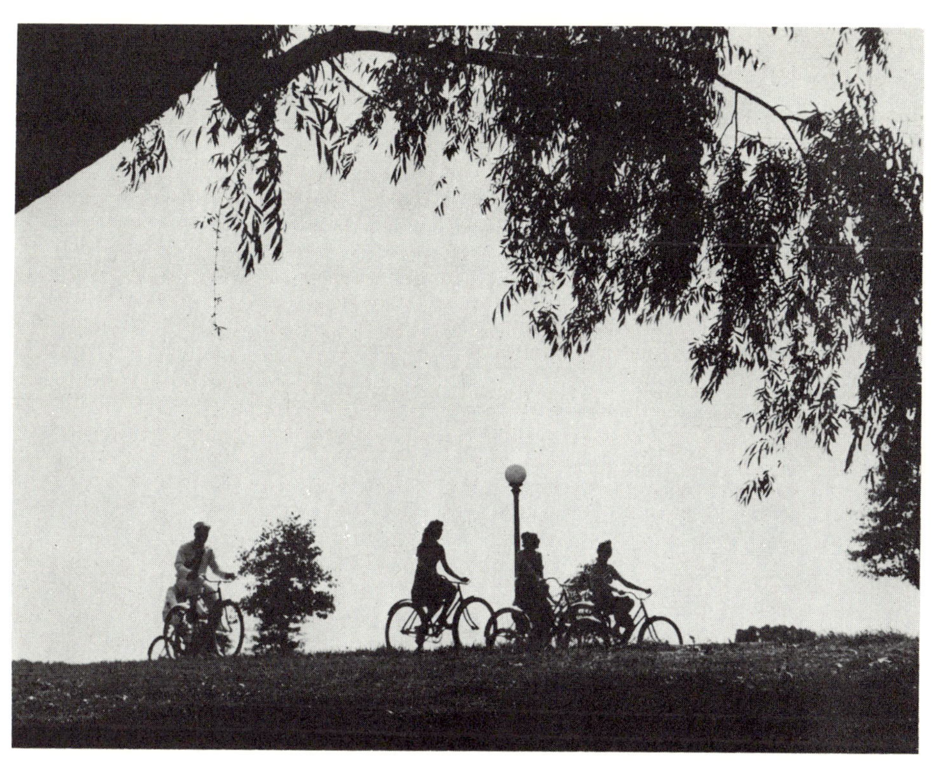

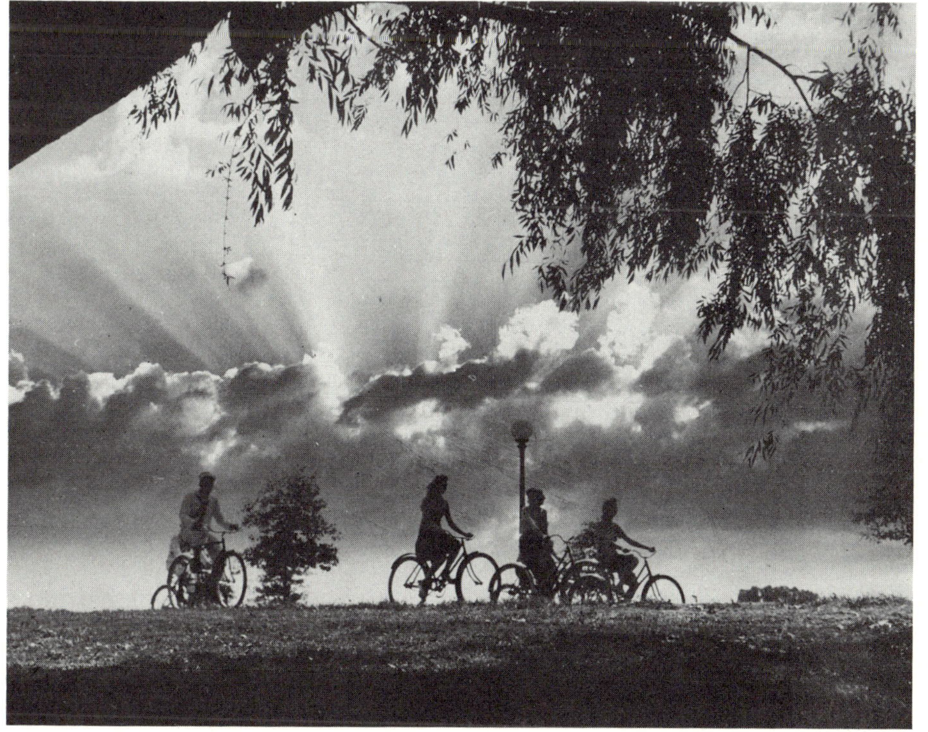

A section of the landscape shown below was combined
with the high contrast face to produce the double print on
the opposite page.

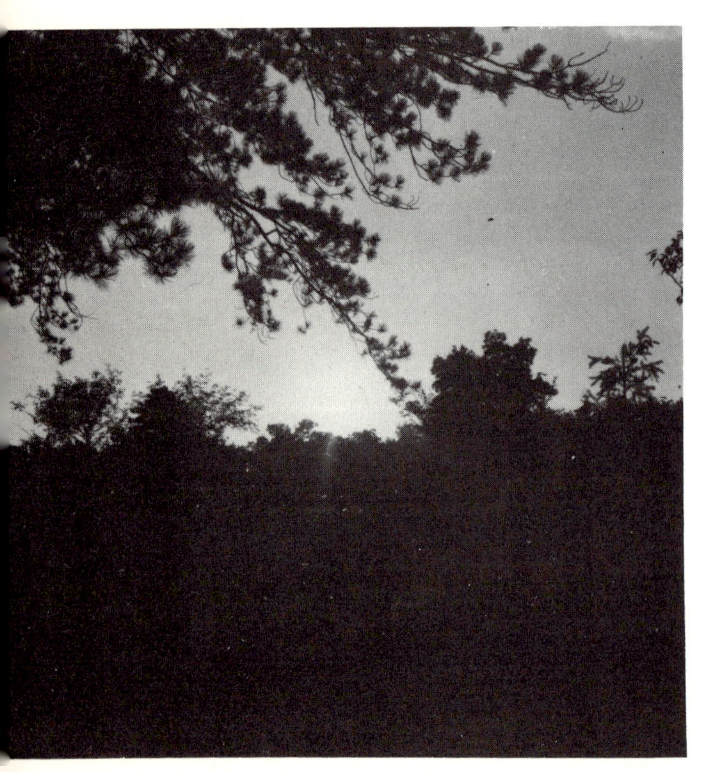

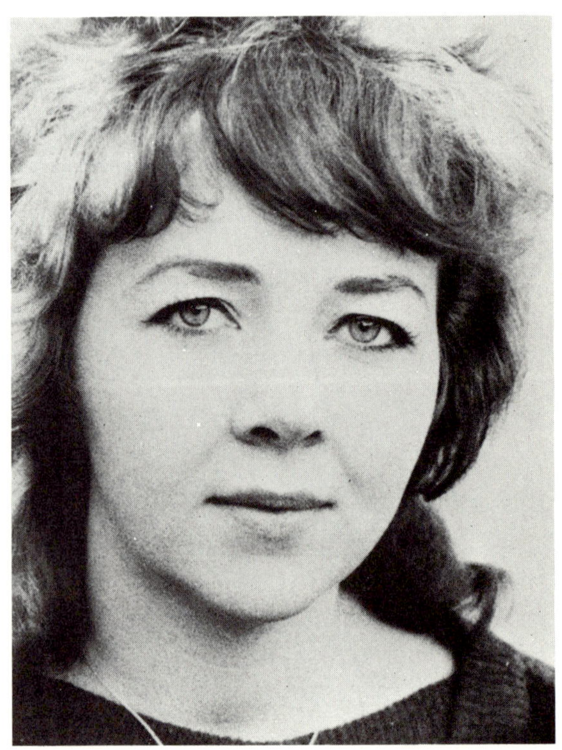

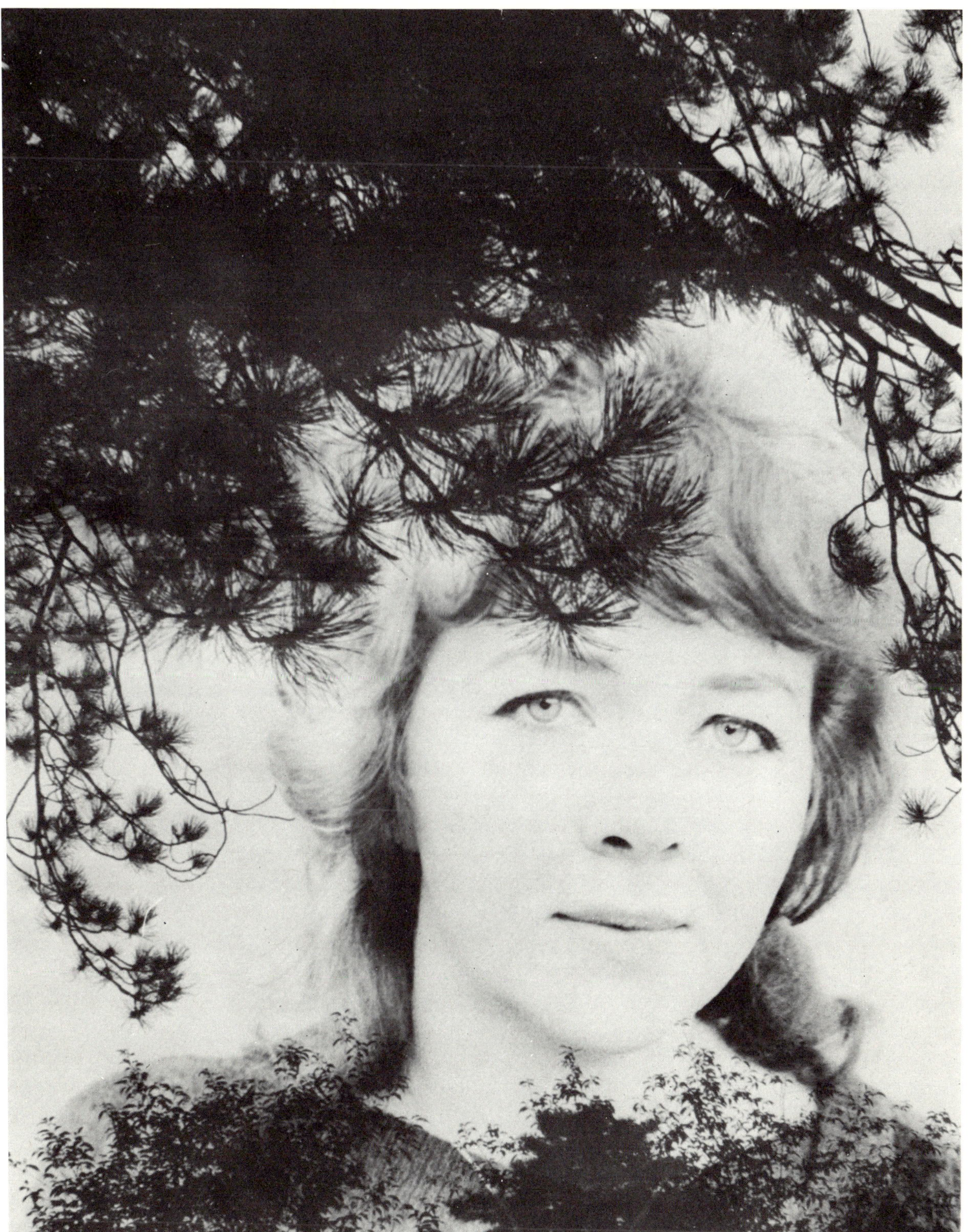

Sharpness is assuredly an asset in most photographs.
However, you may occasionally wish to soften the effect of
your print. This was the case with the print shown at the
top of the opposite page. When a piece of crumpled
cellophane is placed under the enlarger lens, a softer
effect is produced as shown in the center print and in the
detail of the eyes. When a wire-screen diffuser is placed
under the lens as shown below, a similar effect is
produced. The effect of using a texture screen placed
directly on the print is shown in the print and detail shown
at the bottom of the opposite page.

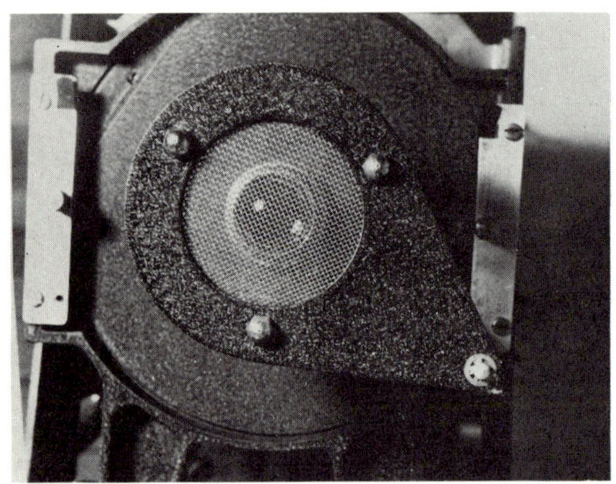

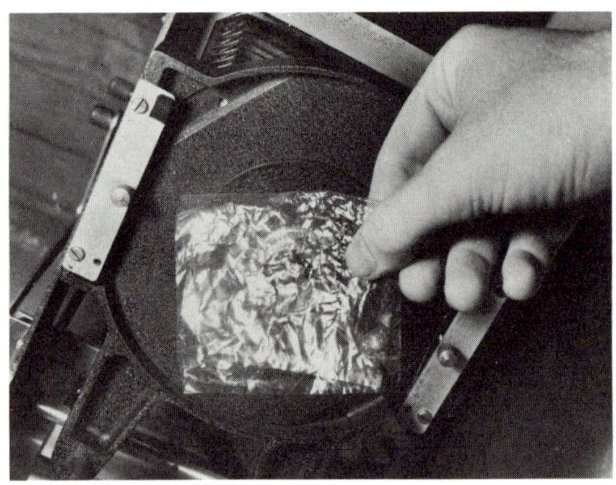

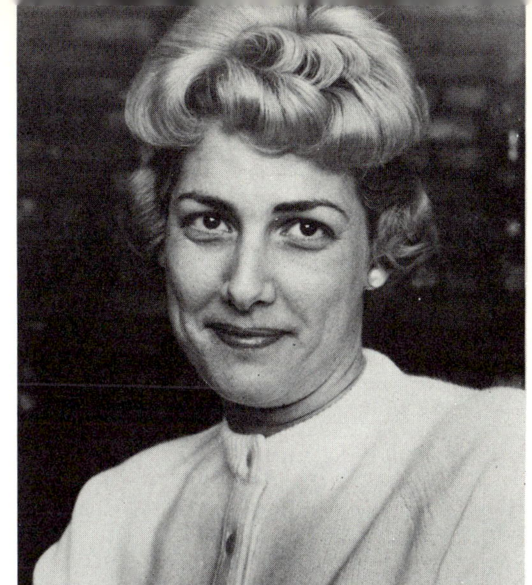

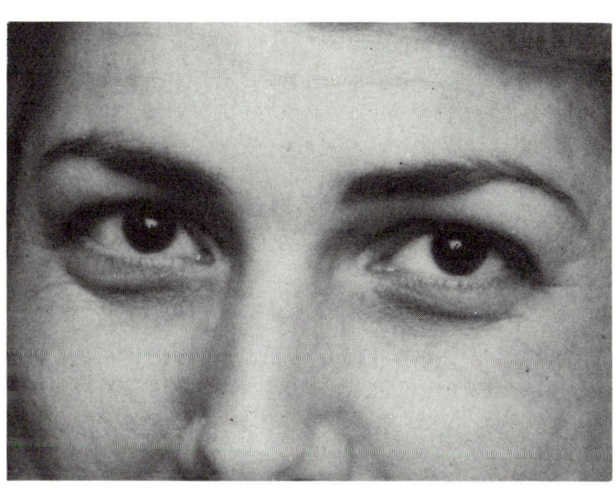

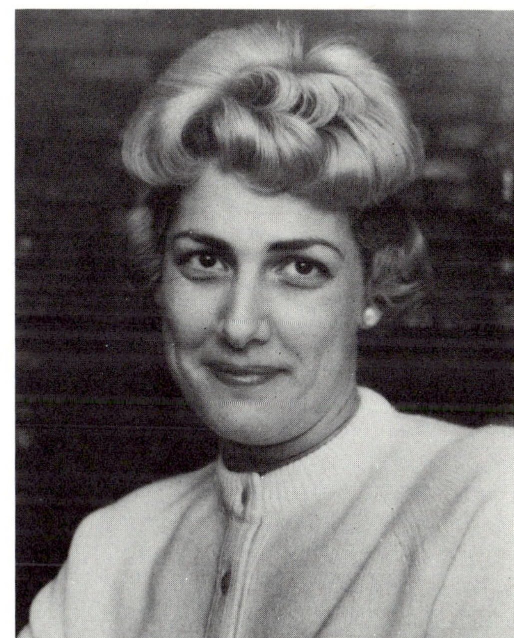

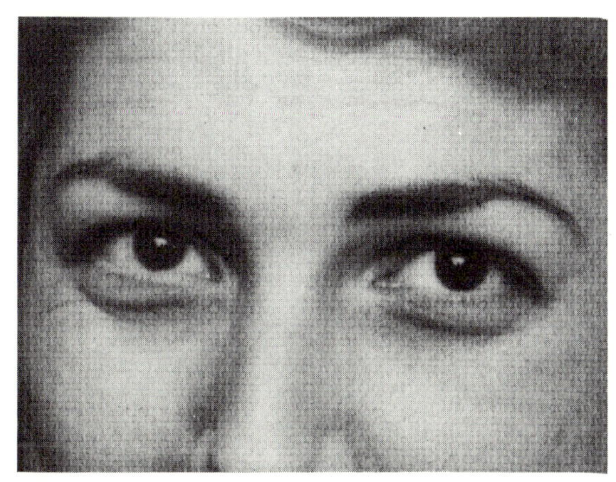

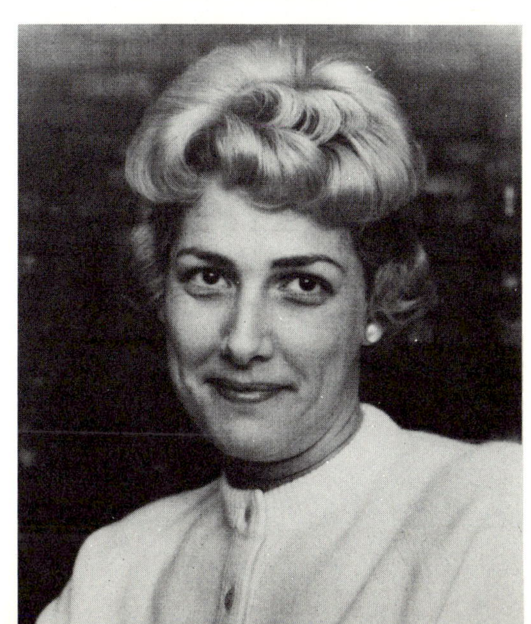

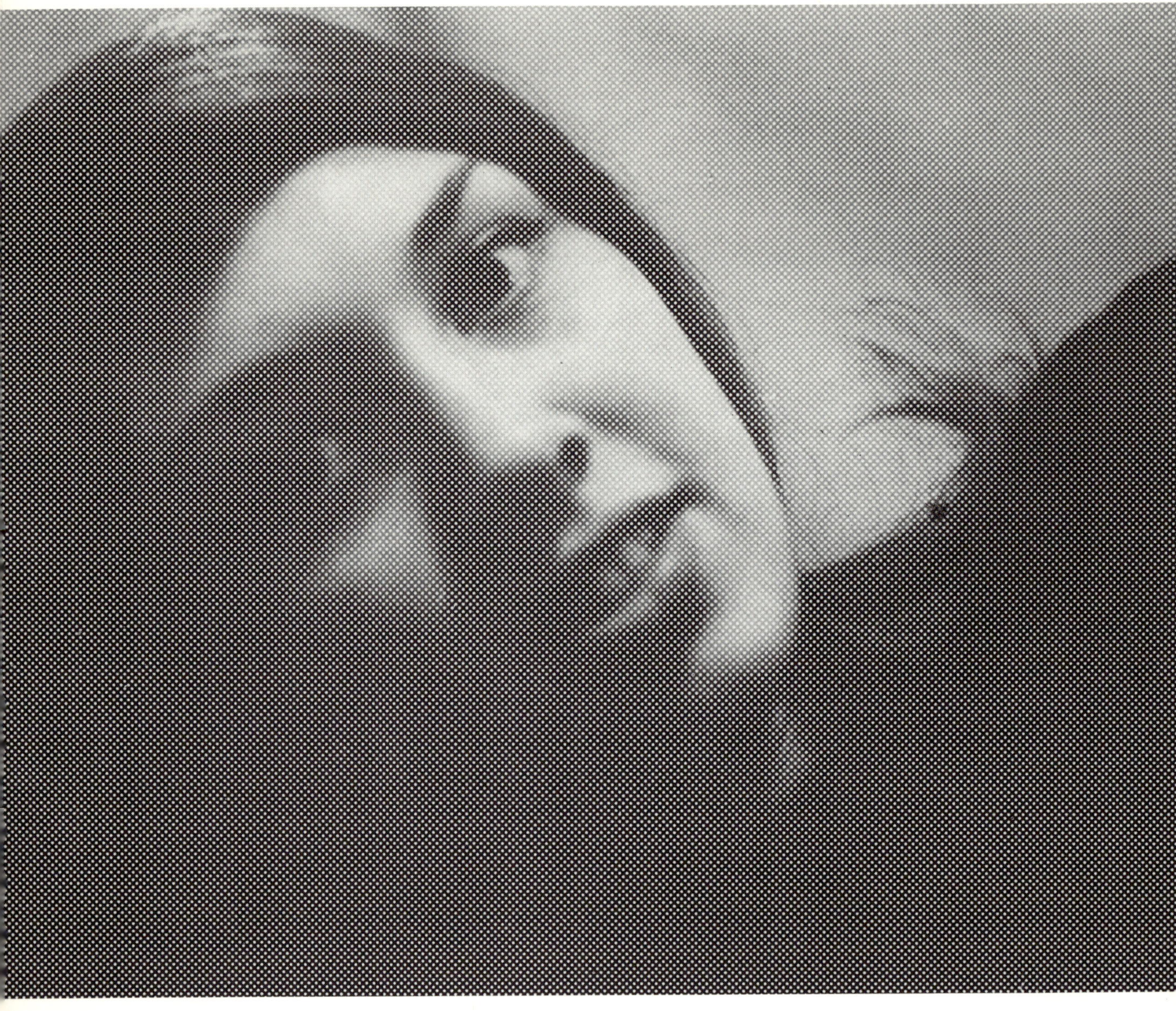

*A more obvious screen effect is shown in this print made
with a dot screen superimposed on the printing paper.*

After your prints have been developed and fixed, it is necessary to wash them completely to remove all traces of the photo chemicals. If these chemicals are not removed the prints will more than likely be spotted or change color at a later date. Therefore, this step is very important for the preservation of your pictures.

Manufacturers of chemicals and papers recommend correct washing times necessary for their products. For best results, follow the instructions. They will vary, but for many printing papers and fixers, one hour washing time is recommended. There are many makes of hypo eliminators or neutralizers on the market. These are intended to cut down on the wash time necessary by removing the hypo chemicals quickly.

Drying of pictures can be accomplished by various methods, ranging from the simple blotter dryers to ferrotype plates or the continuous-action heated drum dryers. The simpler methods are more widely used by most amateurs. Whichever method is used, the process is basically simple.

It is best to start by removing all excess moisture from the pictures. This assures faster drying for all methods. It is especially necessary for ferrotype or drum drying, since it assures good contact between the pictures and the drying surface. This is necessary for best results.

Photographic papers are, of course, coated with an emulsion on one side only. Because these papers have two sides with different rates of drying and different degrees of contraction, they often curl when dry—curling always toward the emulsion. This has to be guarded against almost constantly during the process of drying prints, as curling will cause undue irritation and trouble. This is especially true in winter when humidity is low, since this low humidity also has an effect on the curling of prints. The curved drums of print dryers do not help the situation either.

This is an ongoing problem for the photographer, since it is naturally desirable to turn out finished prints that are flat.

Some photographers have found that when glossy prints are removed from the dryer they will absorb some moisture and will flatten out after a period of time if they are placed on a flat surface. This is especially true in winter in a cool room. This is not a satisfactory solution, however, since the necessary space is not always available. It also requires time for the prints to flatten out by themselves.

Another flattening method is to place a group of prints between two pieces of cardboard and clamp together with clothespins, rubber bands or other type of clamp or fastener that will hold them flat. By placing these prints in a refrigerator while they are in the clamp, they will absorb enough moisture to flatten out. This method works, but it also takes time, and you may also need the refrigerator space.

There is another method of flattening glossy prints that requires no special equipment. It is a method of stretching the emulsion, and curling up the print backwards to counteract the curl of the picture. It is not at all complicated and can be accomplished by either of two different methods. The first method is to place the print flat, on a smooth, hard surface face down and then pass the edge of an ordinary ruler over the back of the print with one hand, while pulling slightly upward on the picture with the other hand. It will be necessary to pass the ruler over the print in one direction, turn the print around and pass it over the surface in the other direction. Repeat this process until the print is satisfactorily straightened. If a ruler is not handy any straight edge that can be handled easily will do.

The second method of straightening is pulling the print downward over the edge of a table with the face of the print facing up. Grasp the print by opposite corners, then slowly but firmly pull it down over the table edge. Follow it over with the hand holding the back of the print. Do this a number of times starting with a different corner each time until the curl has been removed.

One very important point to remember: Do not attempt to use either of these methods of straightening before the print has become cooled from the heat of the dryer. It is best to remove your print from the dryer and allow it to cool slightly, then immediately proceed with the flattening process. If the emulsion is too dry and cold it may be cracked or creased by this process.

Apply the straightening pressure to the print at a slight angle only—regardless of which method you use. Too extreme an angle will also cause cracking of the emulsion. Experience will teach you better than any words can tell.

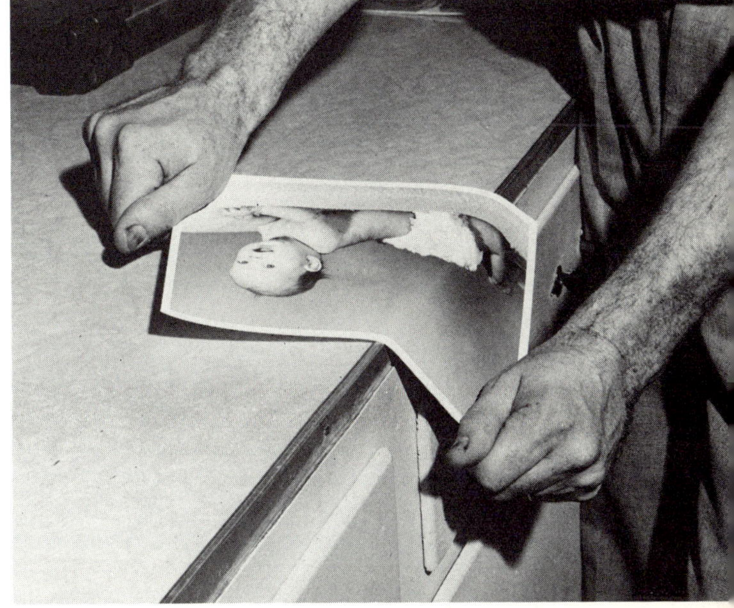

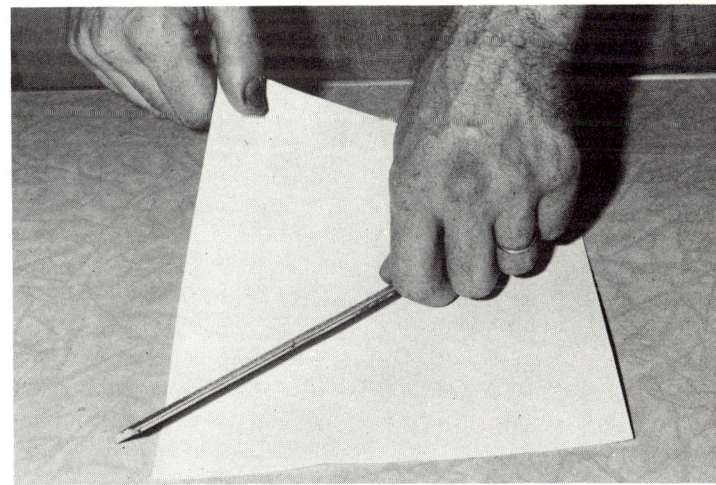

Two methods of straightening curled prints are shown above. You can exert the necessary tension and pressure by pulling the print over the edge of a table with the emulsion side up. With the emulsion side down, you can pull the print up as you pass a metal straightedge across it.

PRINT MOUNTING AND DISPLAY

The effect of your photo prints can be greatly enhanced by the way they are mounted and displayed. Every photographer has his favorite prints and so, doubtlessly, will you. With a little time and even a small budget, you can transform your photos into decorative accessories for your home or office.

Dry Mounting: The best way to mount your prints is by using a material called dry-mounting tissue. The tissue, which resembles waxed paper, is available in art-supply and photo shops. It is placed between the print and backing and when heat is applied, it melts to form a permanent bond.

A special device called a "dry-mounting press" is available and makes mounting your photos a good deal simpler. A flat, temperature-controlled heating element applies the necessary bonding heat to all areas of your photo at once. The tissue can also be used quite successfully with a household iron serving as the heat source.

Only top-quality illustration board should be used as backing for your photos. It is senseless to bother using lesser materials as they will not afford the sturdy reinforcement you hope for.

The mounted print can be trimmed flush to the edge of the picture area so that none of the mounting board shows. If you wish the mount to also serve as a decorative background mat, you must trim the print and tissue and position them exactly on the board before the heat is applied. Once they are mounted, you can display your photos as is by merely pasting a paste-on hook to the backing.

Framing: A good variety of reasonably-priced framing devices are available for your photos. One device that is simplicity itself is simply a shallow plastic box about one inch deep. The print is dropped in face down and a box-filling cardboard form is placed behind it. The back of the cardboard form features pre-punched holes positioned for either vertical or horizontal hanging. A second and slightly more expensive frame is made up of metal strips that are sold in sets of two pieces each. The sets come in all practical lengths so you are not bound by the popular dimensions of pre-cut or made-up frames. The strips are held together with "L" brackets in the corners backed up with a screw-in or push-in locking device. Assembly takes only a few minutes and your photo sports a sleek, yet unobtrusive, frame just like those used to display photos in the finest museums.

DARKROOM DIAGNOSIS

Every photographer, even the best professionals, has had the sad experience of having his high expectations of the shot that seemed so perfect in the taking rewarded with a less than perfect photo. Most often the poor result can be traced to camera malfunction, poor cameramanship, or processing and printing mistakes. Nothing will save that lost picture but as you progress with your darkroom work you will develop the ability to diagnose your results and take the necessary corrective steps.

Camera malfunction, bad shooting techniques, or sloppy darkroom products can be eliminated by a trip to the repairman or greater care on your part in taking your photos and processing them. Many of the photos in the following section illustrate such defects and the captions advise how to avoid them in future work. But, in doing your own darkroom work, you put yourself in the position of not only correcting but also of controlling results. Special techniques are available to you to check and control processing and printing effects as demonstrated on the final pages of this section.

SHUTTER MALFUNCTION

The frames reproduced on this page show the effect of an uneven shutter movement. The frames received less exposure at the right than at the center or left. The only remedy was an expensive trip to the camera repair shop.

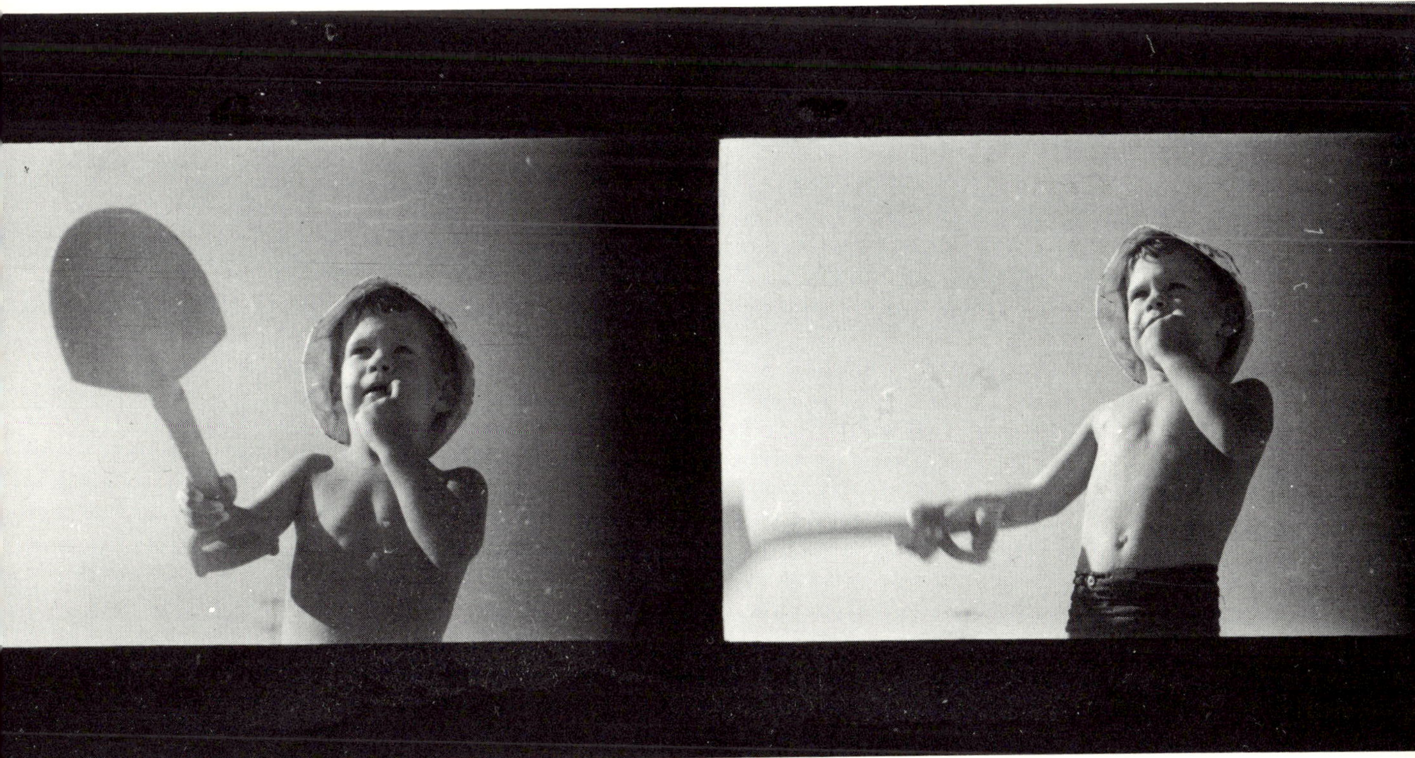

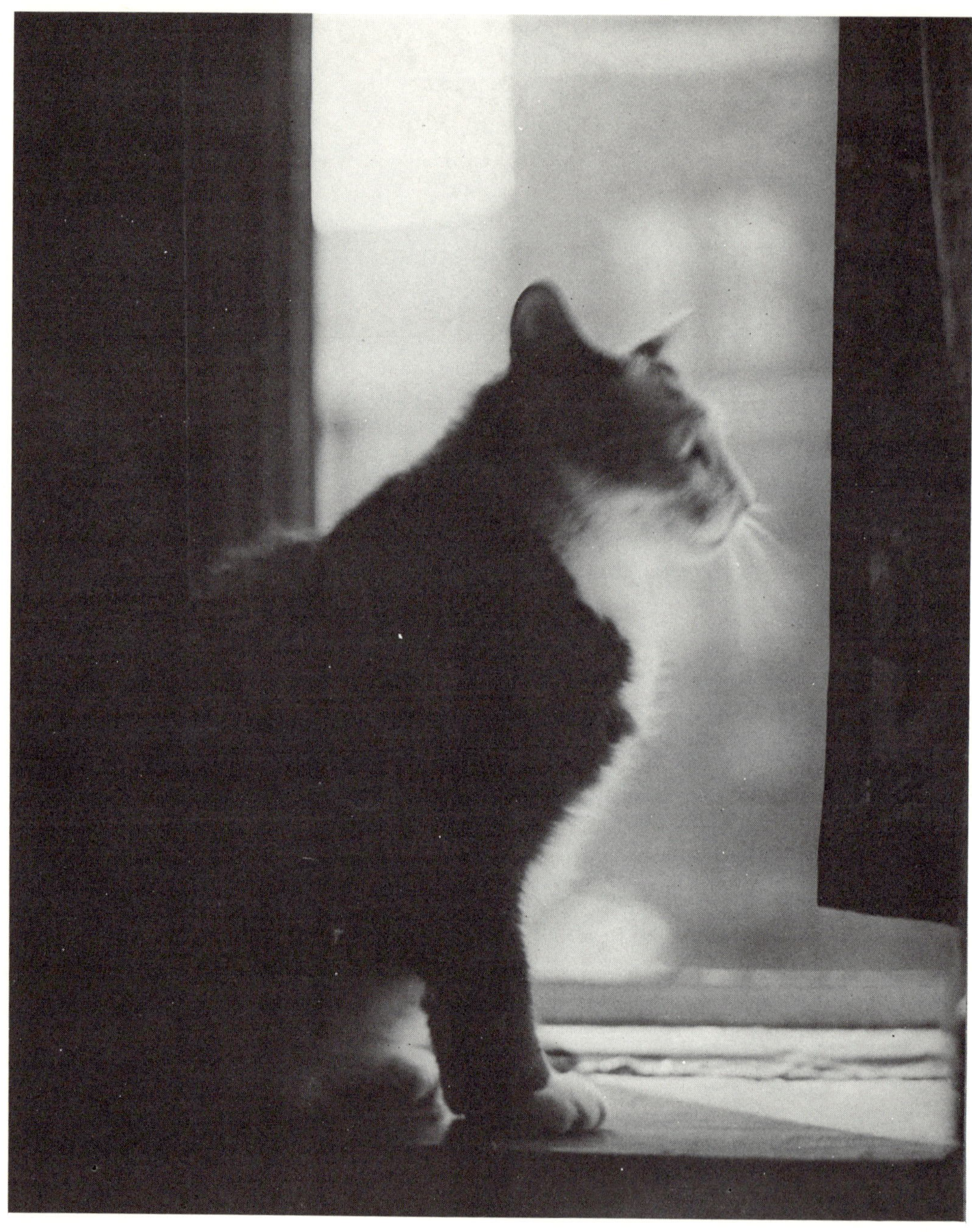

Unless your camera needs serious repair, it will focus on something. Ordinarily, if the focus falls in the wrong place, it is the photographer's fault. In the print above, the curtain, which was slightly closer to the camera than the cat was, is rendered perfectly sharply. Even slight focusing errors are sadly apparent at close shooting distances such as that used for this picture.

In the print below, nothing is sharp. A print such as this must be checked with a magnifier. If the film grain has printed up as distinct specks, nothing can be done to correct the image—the camera wasn't correctly focused. If the grain in the enlargement is not sharply rendered, make another print and this time focus the enlarger more carefully.

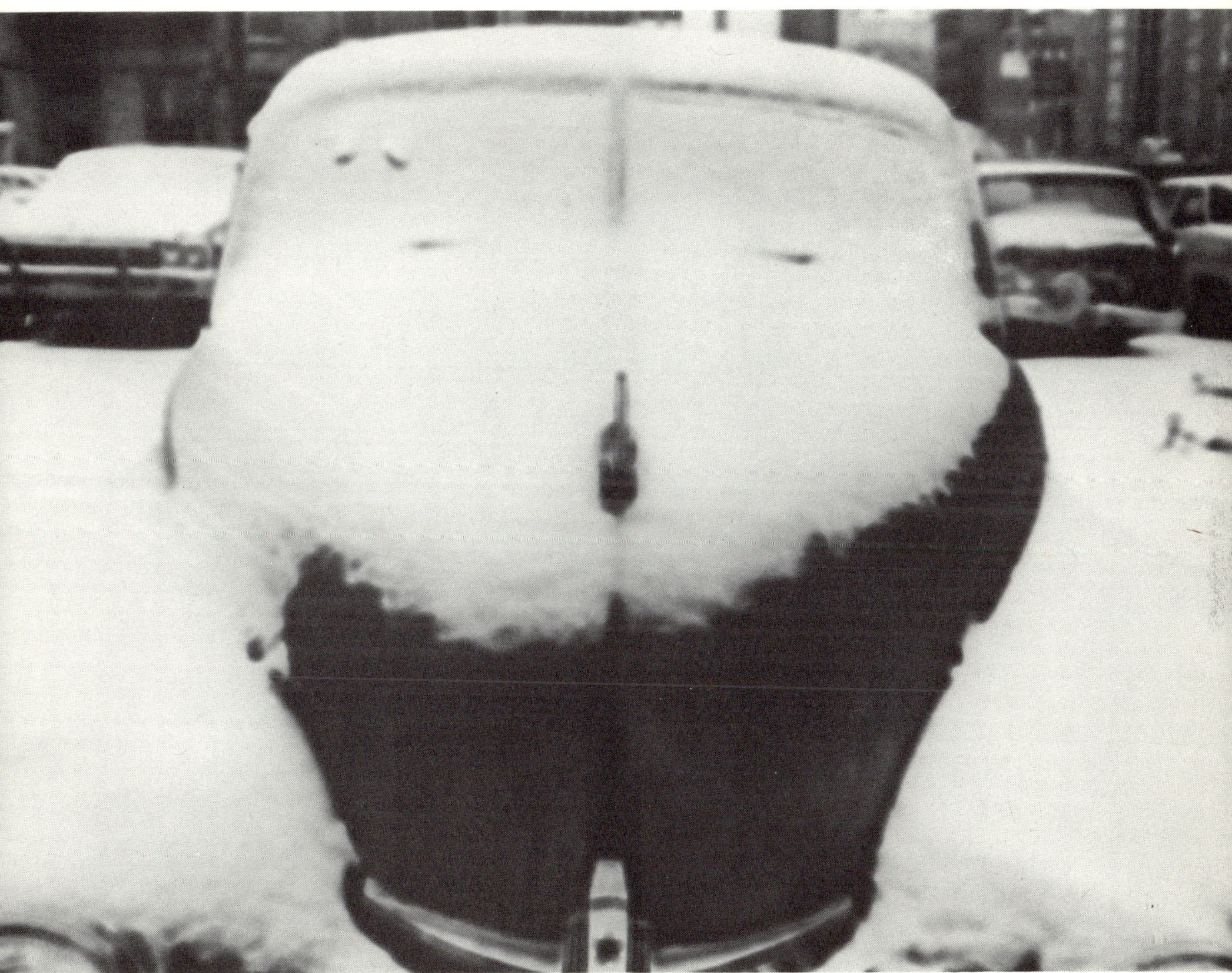

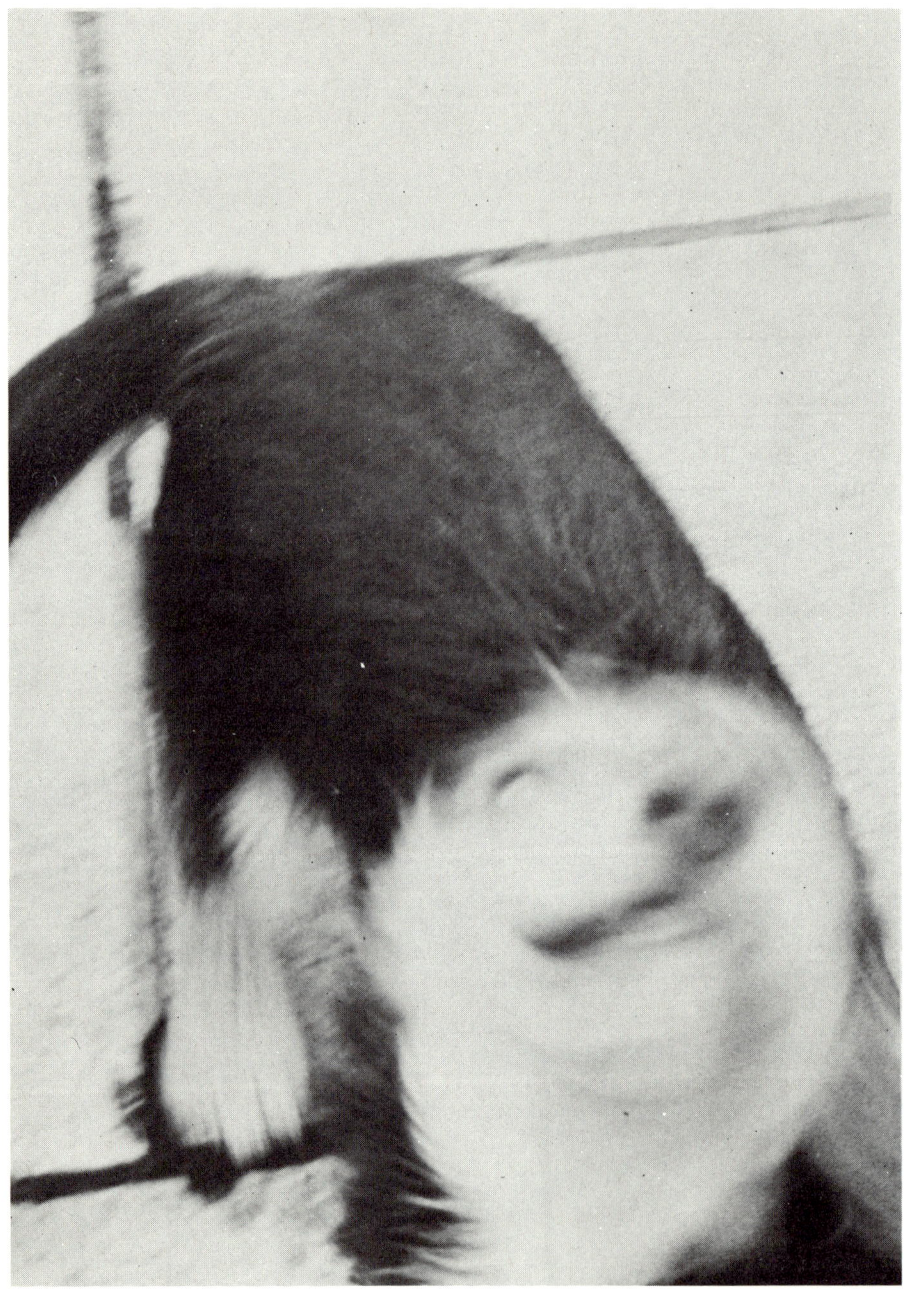

Camera and subject motion combined to produce the blurred image above. Low light necessitated a shutter speed too slow to capture the vivacious subject. And, the photographer moved the camera while shooting—even the background shows blur.

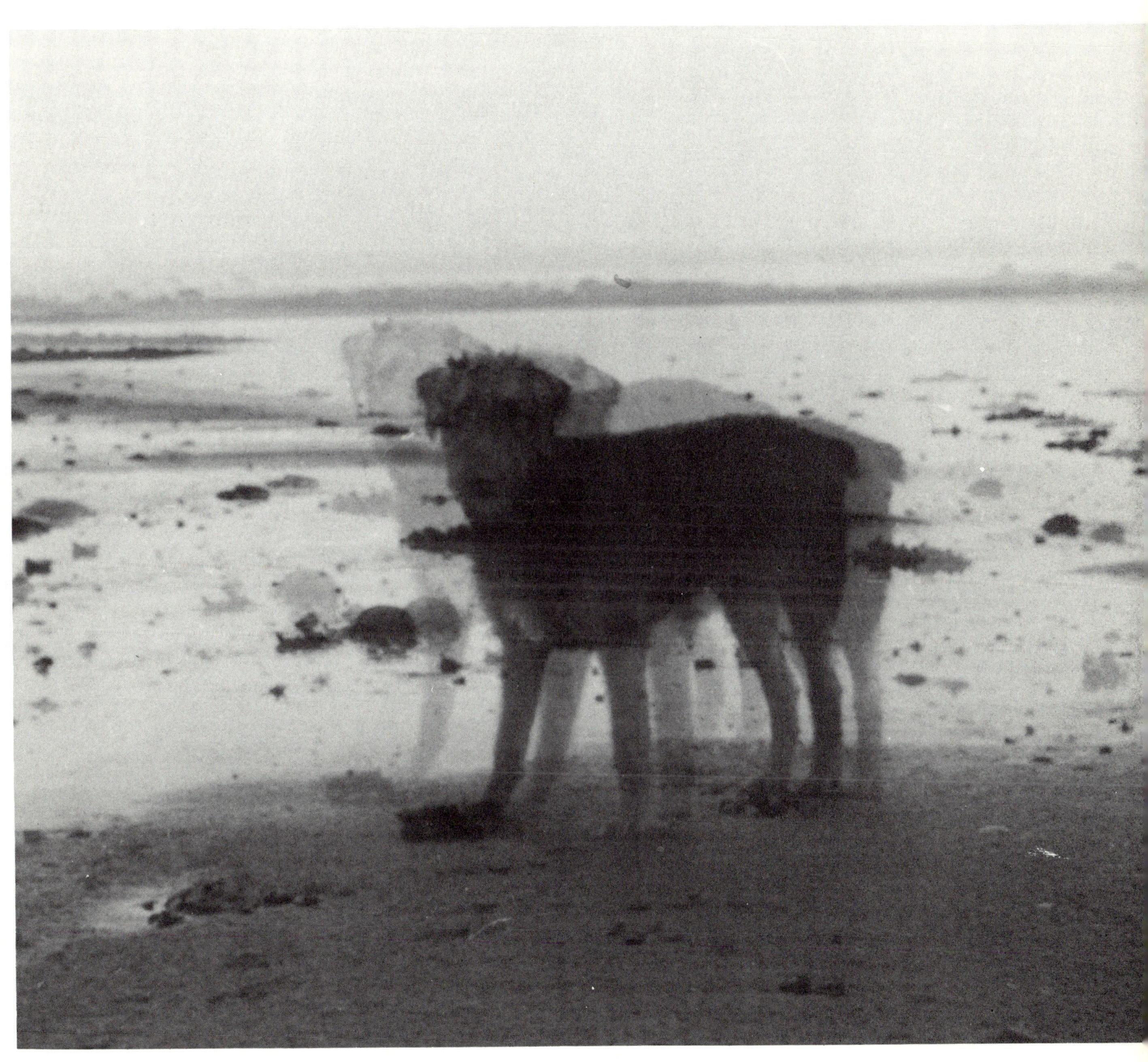

The print above shows the effect of easel motion during the printing exposure. A double image results.

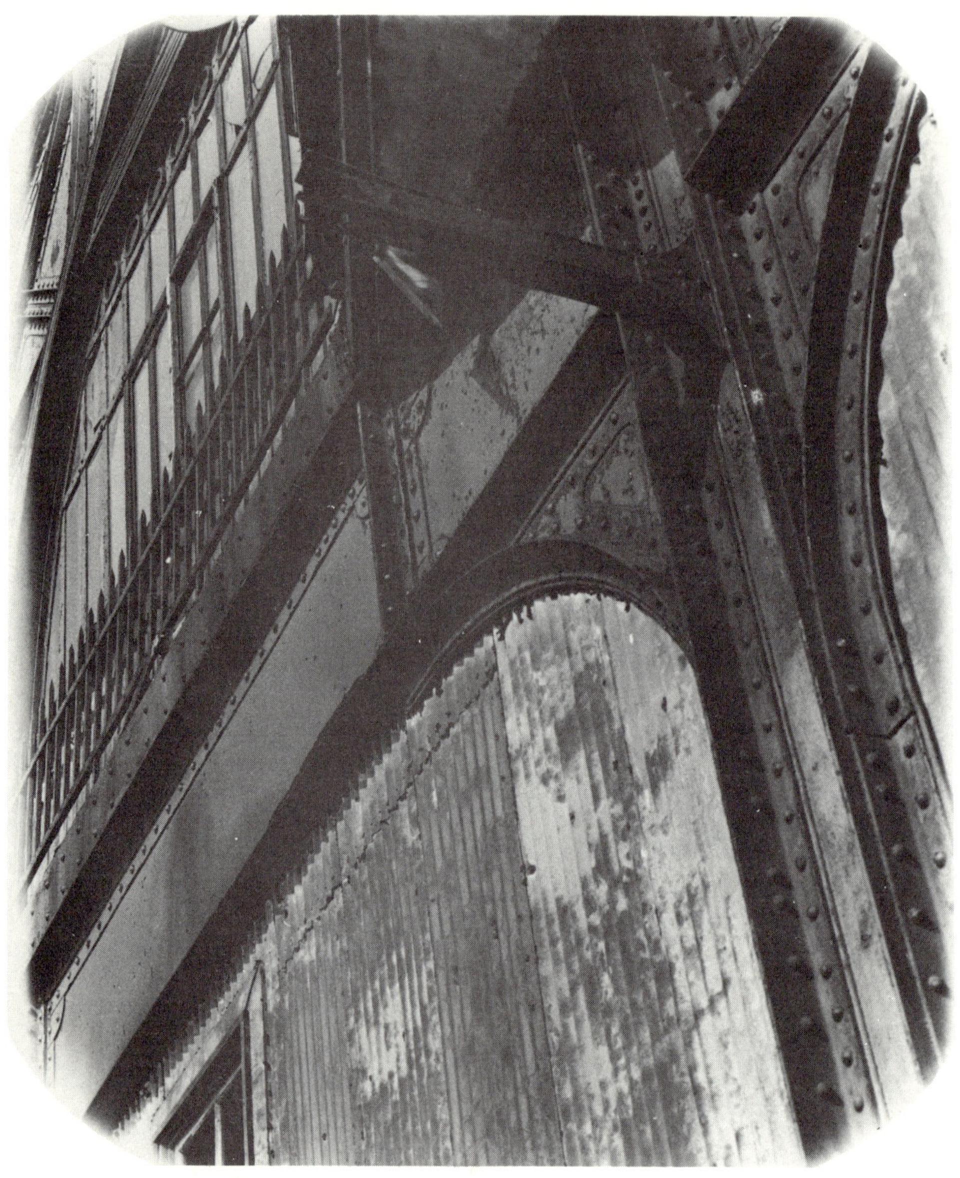

While vignetting is a printing technique, it can also be a shooting or printing fault. The print above has lost its corners in the printing stage. The enlarger condenser and lens were designed for use with 35mm negatives. The print was made from a 120 negative. A similar vignetting can be caused in shooting by the use of a too narrow sunshade or too small filter.

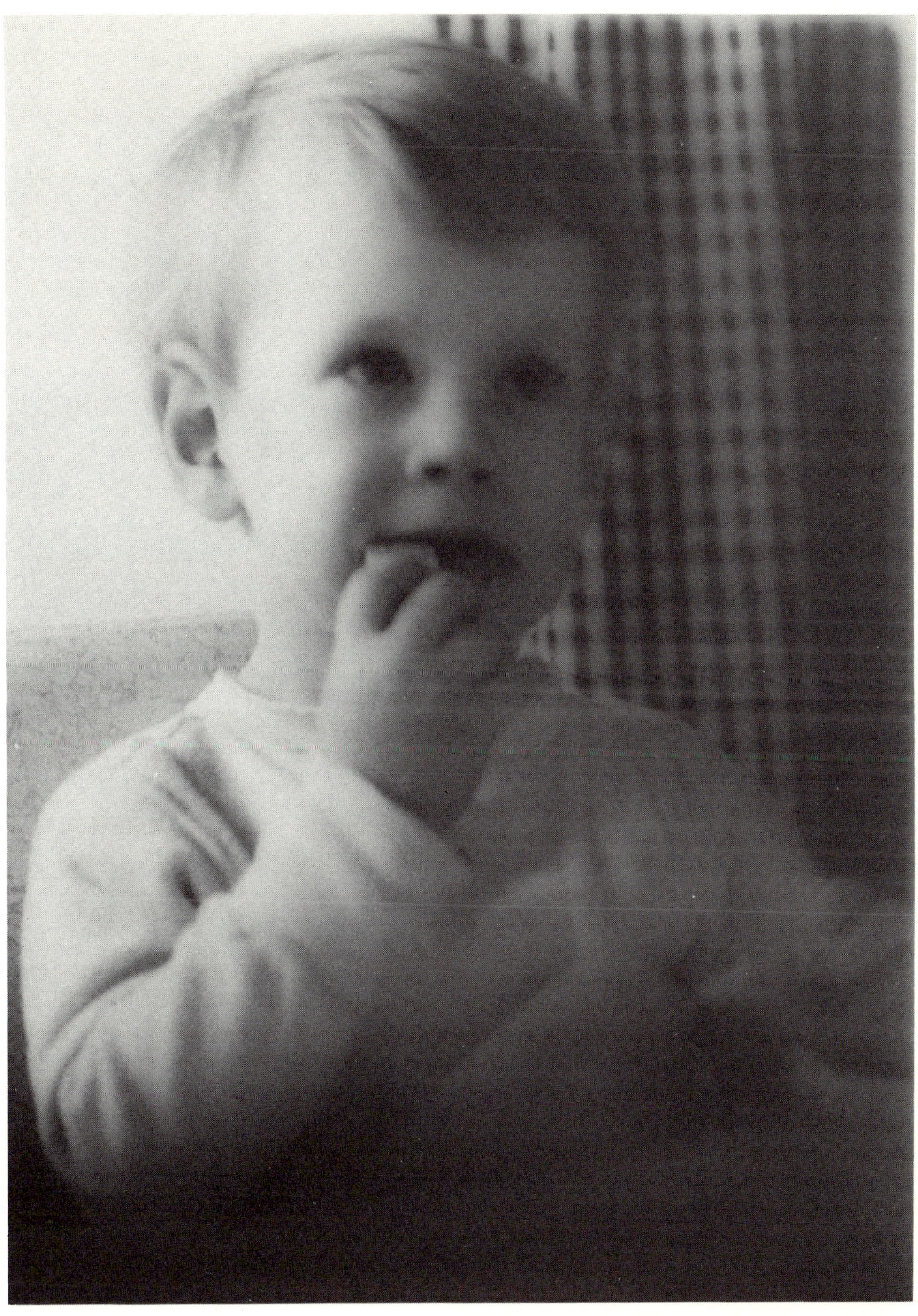

The partially unclear image shown above could be the result of a smudged lens or a dirty shooting or polycontrast filter. Make sure that all lenses and filters are kept scrupulously clean.

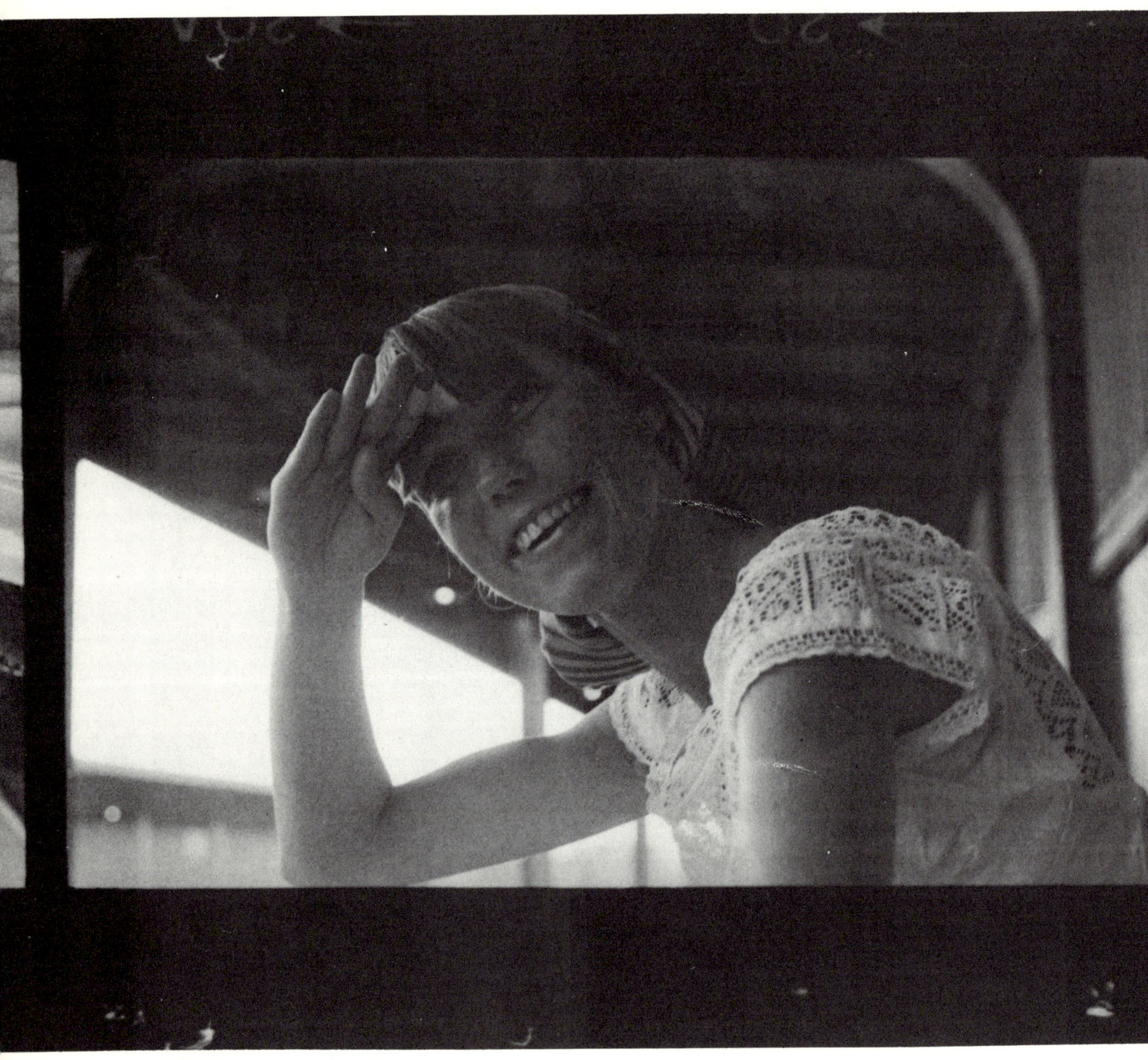

The enlarged contact print shown above displays scratch-es on the subject's neck and arm. White scratches such as these indicate that the damage is to the top side of the negative. Scratches on the emulsion side show up as dark lines in the print. The print on the opposite page shows a chip out of the emulsion. This occurred when the film was washed off the reel after processing.

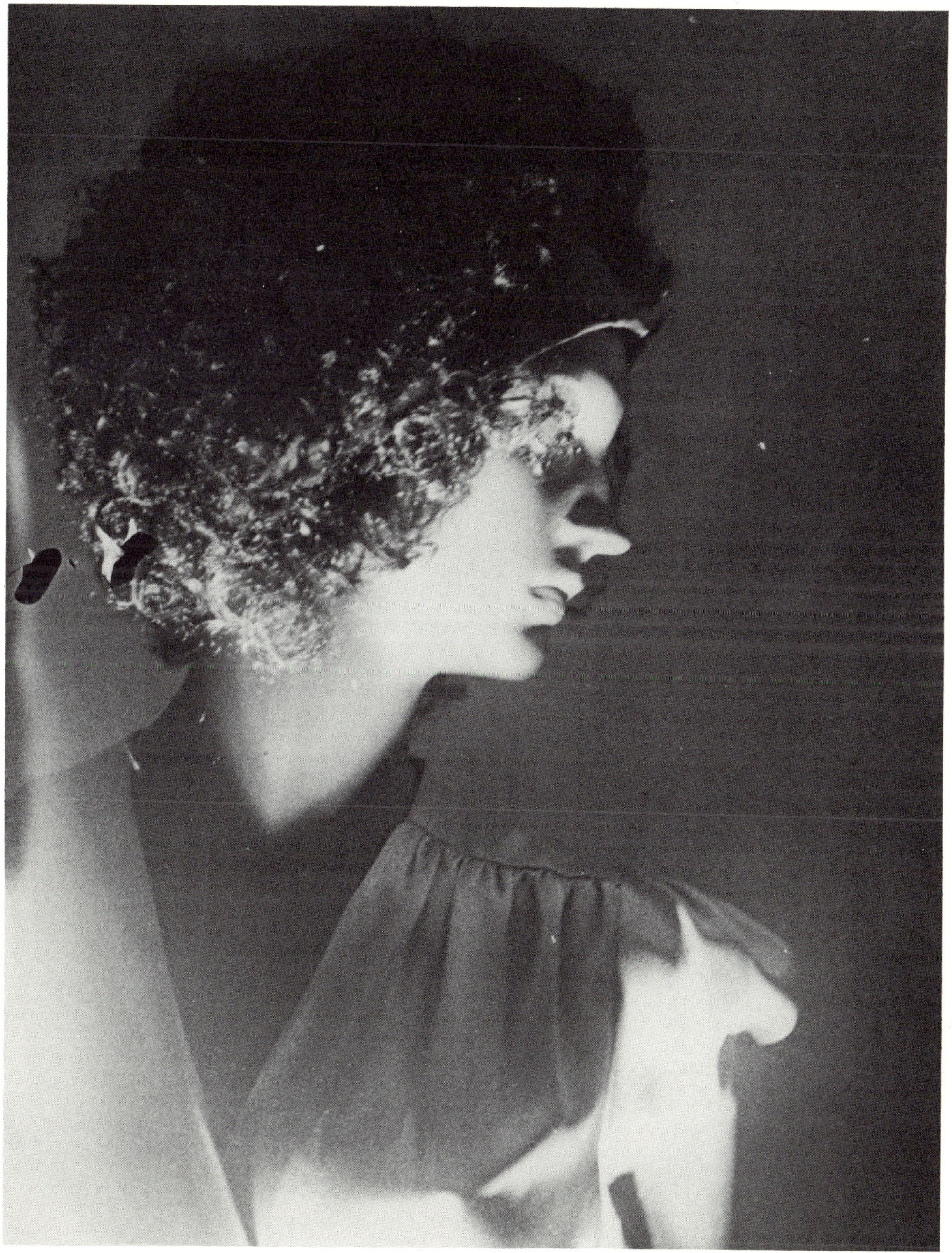

LIGHT-STRUCK (SOLARIZED) NEGATIVES

*The print below was made from a negative that was
accidentally light-struck during processing. While solarization is a respected photographic technique it must be
carefully controlled and is usually performed on duplicate
negatives to guarantee the safety of the original.*

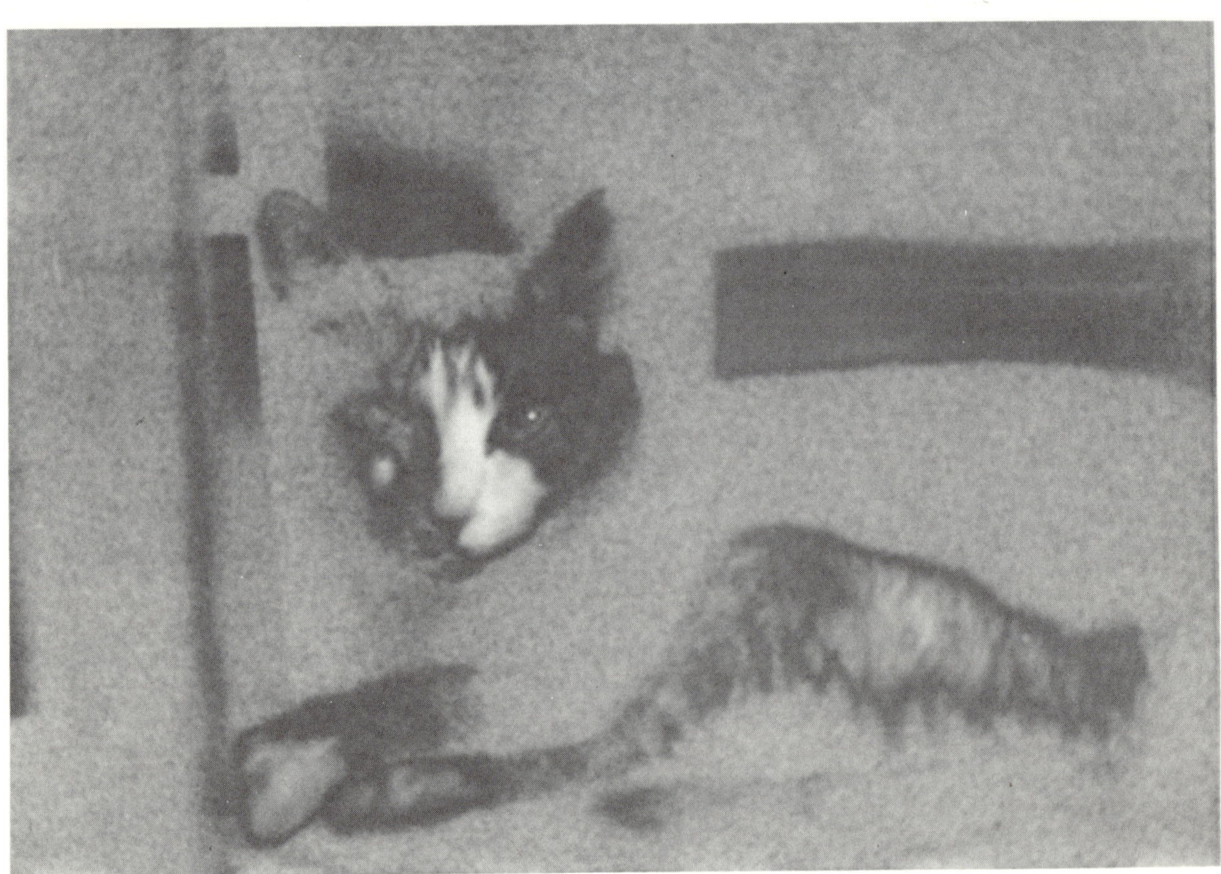

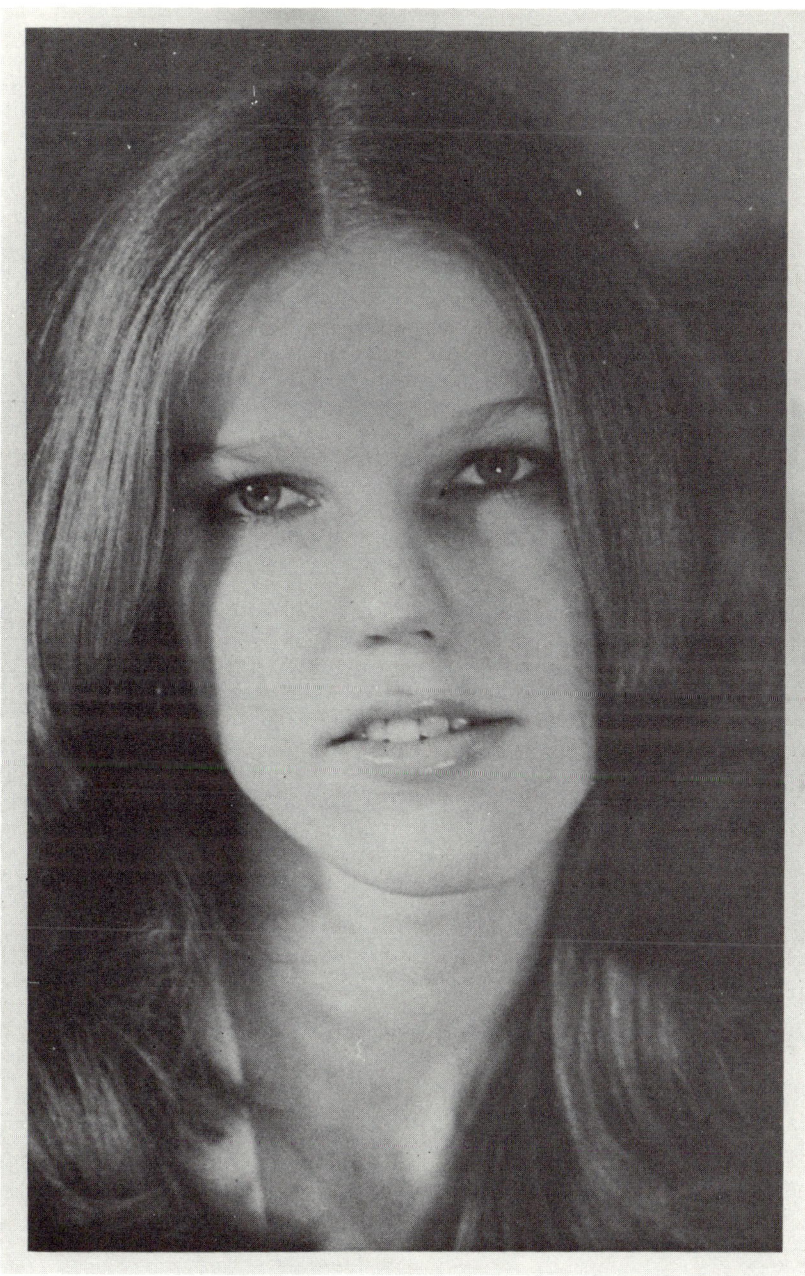

The print above demonstrates the result when printing paper is light-struck or "fogged" during printing or development. The print has no whites and the border is gray.

ERRORS IN DEVELOPMENT

As mentioned earlier, the print must be inserted into the developer with as swift and smooth a gesture as possible. And, the developer must cover all of it. The print below is underdeveloped in the upper left corner because that corner remained out of the developer for part of the development time.

Developer dilution instructions must be followed carefully. A too strong developer will cause the image to come up too rapidly and the tonal range of the print will suffer. This was the case in the print below.

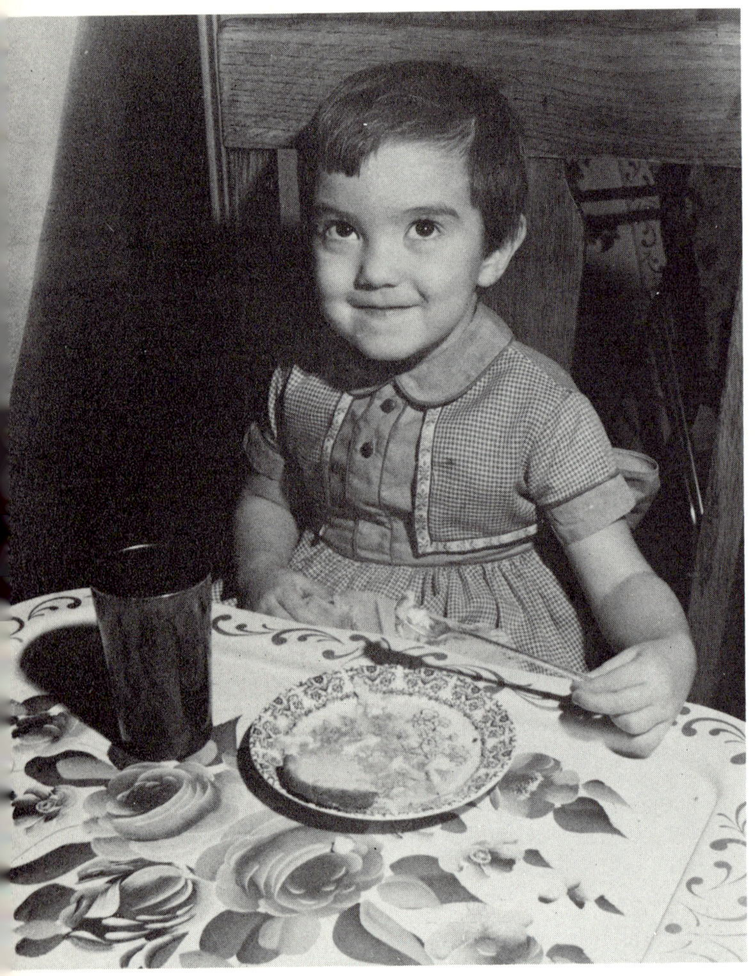

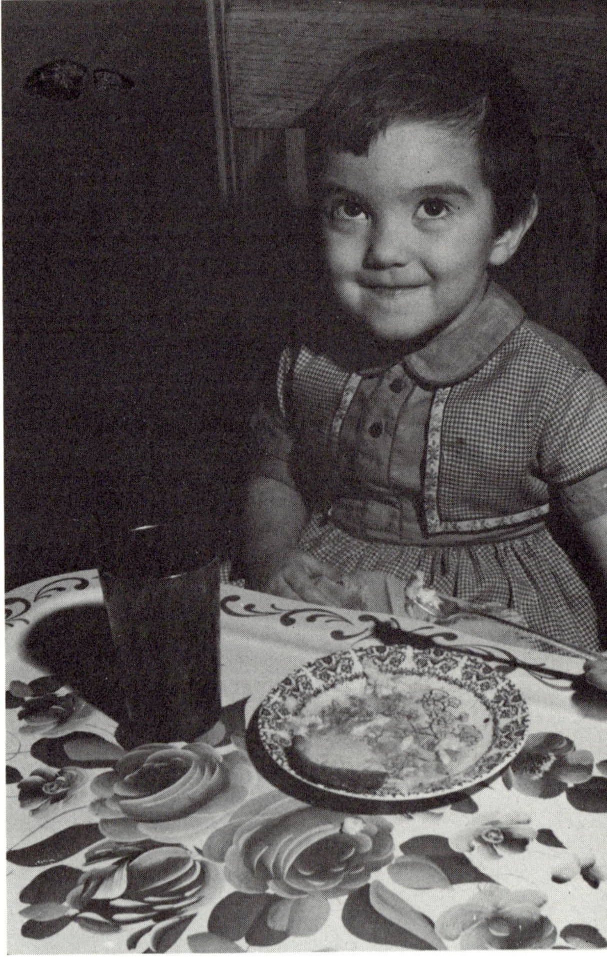

Overzealous agitation during film processing will cause
too much chemical action along the edges of the negative.
The frame below is overdeveloped along the edges. This
accounts for the light edges of the print.

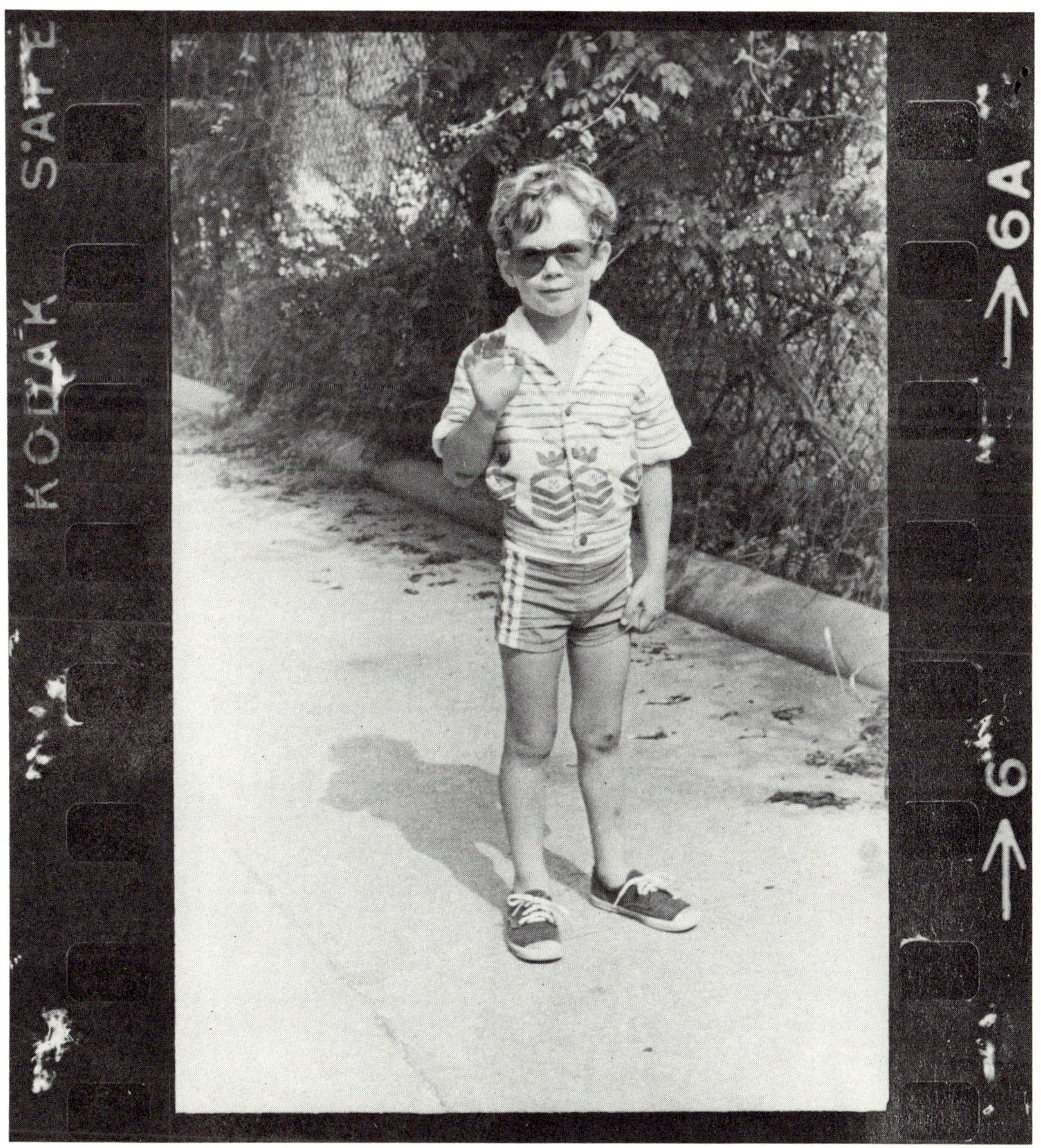

CORRECTIVE "PUSH PROCESSING"

The photos on these pages would not have existed without some foresight on the part of the photographers. Both photos were taken in low-light situations. The film, Tri-X, was deliberately overrated in the exposure to an ASA rating of 1000. Developing time for the film was adjusted to compensate for the relative underexposure.

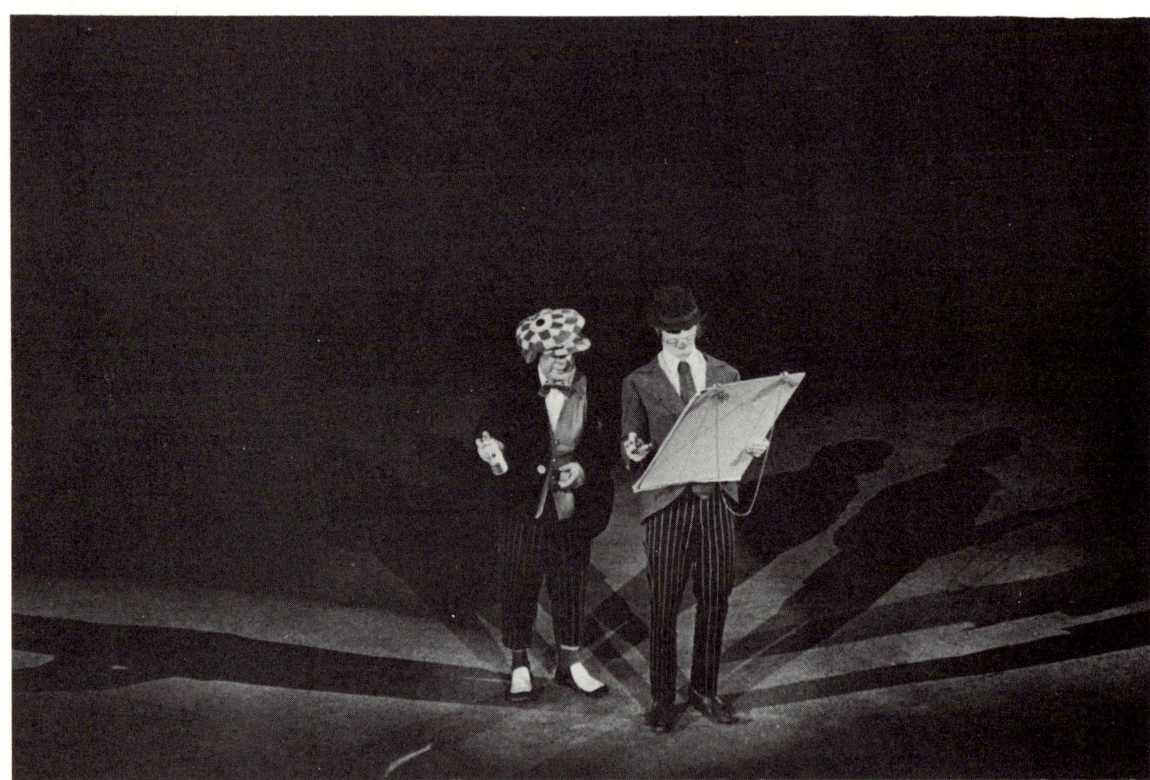

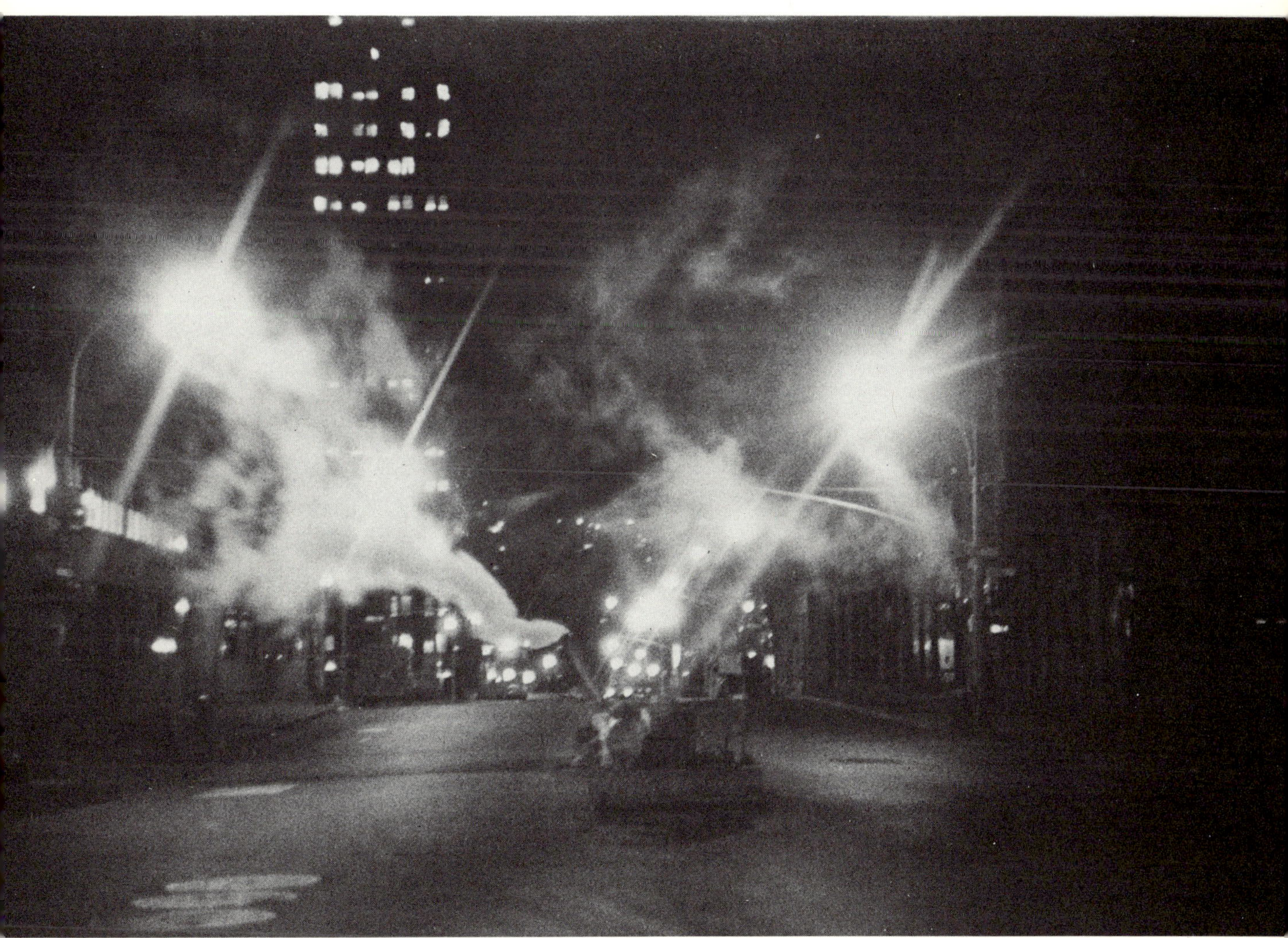

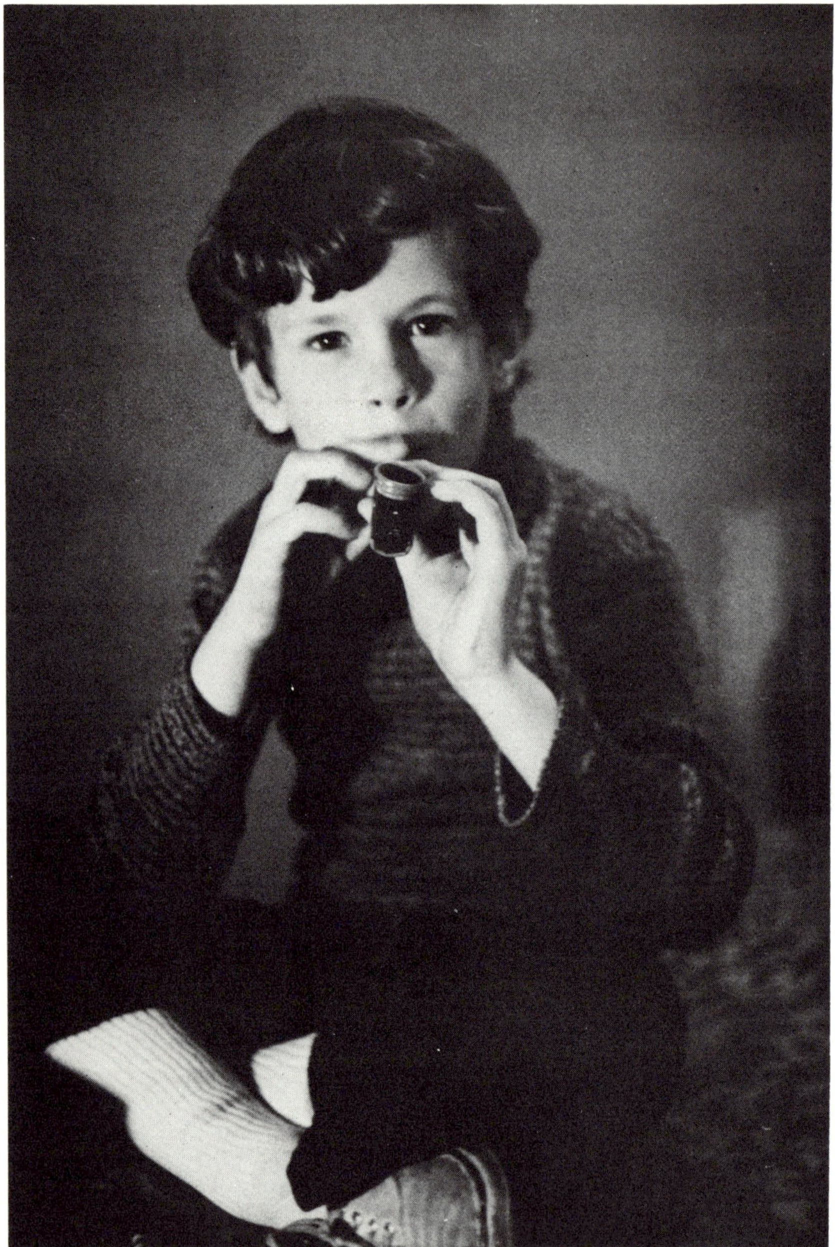

One way to guarantee results when developing your negatives is to clip off a few frames from the start of the roll and process them according to the demands of the original exposure. If the result is satisfactory, you can process the rest of the roll in the same way; if the result is unsatisfactory, the necessary adjustment in time or temperature can be made. The development for the shot above was checked in this way. The picture was taken in very poor light and the photographer did the best she could with the exposure. Rather than risk the whole roll, she made a preliminary clip test to establish developing procedure.

Darkroom work is a pastime that can bring not only better results but also many happy hours to any photographer. With a firm acquaintance with darkroom materials and processes, the amateur darkroom worker can polish his technique into a finely developed craft.

Hopefully, this book has sharpened your interest in darkroom work and provided the information to get you started. Once underway, you will naturally develop an appetite to know more and to go further—essentially, to extend your techniques beyond the limits of what has been described here. There are many fine books available to help you satisfy this craving. Especially recommended are *Darkroom Techniques, Volumes 1 and 2* by Andreas Feininger (Amphoto, 1973). These fully illustrated books have been prepared by one of the world's most famous photographic writers. In them, Mr. Feininger displays his fine triple talent—in photography, in darkroom procedures, and in clear, concise writing. Principles for both routine and creative techniques are described.

Also available for those who wish to explore darkroom image manipulation are *Darkroom Magic* by Otto Litzel (Amphoto, 1967, 1974), *The Creative Darkroom* (Eastman Kodak Company, 1973), and *Solarization* by Sandy Walker and Clarence Rainwater (Amphoto, 1974).

Now, lights out and to work.